2
WASHINGTON SQUARE

Constance Congdon

*based on the novel by
Henry James*

BROADWAY PLAY PUBLISHING INC
New York
www.broadwayplaypublishing.com
info@broadwayplaypublishing.com

Cover photo compliments of Ron Bashford and Amherst College Department of Theatre & Dance.

First edition: November 2020
I S B N: 978-0-88145-846-6

Book design: Marie Donovan
Page make-up: Adobe InDesign
Typeface: Palatino

2 WASHINGTON SQUARE is based on Henry James'
novel, *Washington Square*. The play was co-conceived
and developed with Ron Bashford.

The original production was by the Amherst College
Department of Theatre & Dance in the Kirby Memorial
Theater, 27-29 October 2011. The cast and creative
contributors were:

DR ELEANOR SLOPER..Lexa Gluck
CATHERINE SLOPER ....Michelle Escobar
MRS LAVINIA PENNIMAN .... Alexandra Constas
ARTHUR TOWNSEND .... David Baird
MORRIS TOWNSEND................................Justin Knoll
MARIA...Maria Kirigin

Director...Ron Bashford
Costume design.................................Javier Chavez Chacon
Lighting design... Kathy Couch
Set design.. Nora Smith
Sound design....................................... Stephanie Robinson
Stage manager.. Jeffrey Moro

CHARACTERS & SETTING

DR ELEANOR SLOPER, *a physician, OB-GYN, age 40, very WASPy*

CATHERINE SLOPER, *her daughter, age 18, looks like her father who was Cuban*

MRS LAVINIA PENNIMAN, ELEANOR's *sister, a widow, age 43, WASPy but naive*

ARTHUR TOWNSEND, *a family friend, age 45, from an old, white N Y C family*

MORRIS TOWNSEND, *a cousin of* ARTHUR's, *age 26. He is of mixed race, as is* CATHERINE, *and looks like his mother who was a French black woman.*

MARIA, *a domestic servant, young 30s, has been with the family since* CATHERINE *was 8 or 9. She is Italian and looks dark.*

Place: The entire action of the play takes place in the front parlor of DR ELEANOR SLOPER's *house on Washington Square, New York City.*

Time: 1960–1965

ACT ONE

Scene One

(Early evening, interior of Dr Eleanor Sloper's *home, a well-appointed brownstone In the prestigious area of Washington Square, New York City. It is October and the leaves have turned. Eisenhower's Vice-President, Richard Nixon, has lost his bid for the Presidency to John F Kennedy.* Eleanor *supported Nixon, but was too busy to spend time on political campaigns, as she is continung to maintan her successful Park Avenue gynecology practice.* Eleanor *enters and is met by* Maria, *the maid).*

Eleanor: People are arriving any minute now and I have to change. Where's the mail? Oh, nevermind. I have one of my headaches, anyway. Take my briefcase, Maria.

Where is my daughter?

Maria: She's upstairs, putting on her dress.

Eleanor: Did the dressmaker do a good job? It has to fit well. She's quite curvy, my daughter. The Jews would call it "zaftig". She's built like all Spanish women, the peasants, anyway. Although her father was…tall. You never met him, of course. But you've seen the photos.

Maria: Yes, Ma'am.

Eleanor: Lavinia was quite stunned when she met him. She was so certain that her "catch", the perfect minister, was the most beautiful man. Beautiful and godly. He was insufferable. The Right Honorable Reverend Penniman had "attachments" to women in his congregation. Poughkeepsie wouldn't pay for a second pastor so HE was the Minister of Visitation, comforting widows. And Poughkeepsie is quite *cold*, lots of *cold* winter evenings. Lavinia at home, embroidering. I should have more compassion for her. But, at least, she had her husband for years. *Where is Catherine?*

MARIA: Shall I go get her?

ELEANOR: No. Fix me a drink. And some headache powder and soda.

MARIA: The bar has been moved to the garden.

ELEANOR: Why!?? Oh, for the guests.

LAVINIA: *(Entering from upstairs)* Oh, Eleanor! I thought I heard you. Listen, the dress at the dressmaker—well, the color. Neither Catherine nor I liked the color. I mean, sage green did nothing for her. Maria, can you help Miss Catherine? She needs help with her hair. And you know how to do it.

(MARIA *looks at* ELEANOR *for what to do,* ELEANOR *okays* MARIA *going upstairs to help* CATHERINE)

ELEANOR: So, what are you telling me?

LAVINIA: I took her shoppIng.

ELEANOR: She bought somethIng off the rack?

LAVINIA: We had to look, but she found this dress.

ELEANOR: At Bergdoff-Goodman.

LAVINIA: No.

ELEANOR: Lord and Taylor, then.

LAVINIA: Orbach's

ELEANOR: Why not Gimbel's or Macy's or the Sears and Roebuck catalog? Orbach's is wholesale so-called fashion! How, Lavinia, how am I to get my daughter married off to anyone who is anybody if she won't bother to dress in a way that is flattering to her and worthy of her status in society?? She shows no interest in a career. Of course, you passed on your invaluable talent in embroidery and needlework. Oh, this headache.

LAVINIA: Your daughter excels in skills that are the most valued for a woman. She's been managing this household since she came home from Vassar.

ELEANOR: She barely began her major In Obsolete French—

LAVINIA: Medieval French, Eleanor. With a concentration on pastoral poetry.

ELEANOR: And what did she think she could she do with a degree in pastoral poetry? Become a shepherdess? Why didn't I send her to Barnard? Mount Holyoke? Smith? Away from Poughkeepsie.

LAVINIA: Poughkeepsie is a fine community. Why does everyone put Poughkeepsie down? Poor Poughkeepsie.

ELEANOR: If you love Poughkeepsie so much, go back there and live, Lavinia!

LAVINIA: Ellie!

ELEANOR: Oh God, don't cry. Liv. Liv. You know this is your home. And you're the only one who can get through to Catherine. Oh, my head is pounding.

LAVINIA: I love her. You have no idea how good she is and how much she wants to please you.

ELEANOR: *Too eager to please.* She's so…spineless! That's why I couldn't send her to Smith or Mount Holyoke! I was so certaIn she'd be led astray by some man. Some farmer from the University of Massachusetts or, worse yet, some rake from Amherst College. Who would never marry her. You know how they are.

LAVINIA: No, I don't, Eleanor.

ELEANOR: Of course you don't. I am the only one in this household who knows anything about the world! If her father had lived, all this struggle… Oh, I still would have had a daughter. *(Beat)* Well, we can't dwell in the past. When is Arthur arriving?

LAVINIA: In about fifteen minutes.

ELEANOR: I have to change. I'm going to check on the catering first. That damned baby made me so late. These women all smoke to stay thin, and they have these underweight infants. But he'll be fine. Grow up to take his place in the world. He's a Vanderhooven— haven-or something. Georgina and…Binky, whatever the husband's first name is. When Arthur comes, have him bring me a drink, wherever I am at the time.

(ELEANOR exits towards the kitchen which leads to the garden. After a beat, MARIA enters from upstairs)

MARIA: Miss Catherine wanted me to check to see if her mother is still down here.

LAVINIA: She's headed to the kitchen. And then she's going upstairs to change for the evening.

MARIA: Miss Catherine didn't want to have to make an entrance, just, in case, her mother didn't like—

LAVINIA: Her mother will stop in the garden to make herself a martini. And then she'll take the backstairs from there. Trust me. And she's got one of her headaches, so that will take some time because she'll have to find her medicine in her bathroom. You usually make it for her and you are otherwise engaged helping us.

CATHERINE: *(From the head of the stairs)* Is it clear?
Mother's gone?

LAVINIA: Yes, dear. It's safe.
Come on. I promise you the coast is clear.

*(CATHERINE comes down the stairs. She's in a new red dress
and MARIA has done her hair. She looks striking, but over
the top in terms of tastefulness).*

CATHERINE: Is it too…red? It's awfully red. It's redder
than it looked in the store.

LAVINIA: It's…

CATHERINE: Oh Gosh. Mother will hate it.

LAVINIA: You don't know that.

CATHERINE: I do. I've lived with her for all my life.
You've only been here a few months.

LAVINIA: We were children together, Catherine.

CATHERINE: My mother was never a child. She was
born full-grown.

LAVINIA: She was a lovely child… Well, "lovely" may
be the wrong word. She was beautiful. Always.

CATHERINE: You were, too, Aunt Lavinia.

LAVINIA: No, dear. I was…nice. I was the "nice one" —
not the smart one, nor the beautiful one. And I was the
big sister who married well, at least, until your mother
married your very romantic father. He was so dark and
handsome. Cuban. Like that man on "I Love Lucy."
But dignified. *(To MARIA)* Thank you, Maria.

(MARIA exits.)

CATHERINE: What else can I wear?? I have my
graduation dress, but that dress was too sad, Mother
thought. And I agree. The dressmaker picked the navy
blue, because it was slimming. Oh no. And now this
dress is too tight. I can't breathe, Aunt Lavinia!

LAVINIA: You're upset. That's why you can't breathe. Come to me. Calm down and take a deep breath. I'll hold you. *(She holds* CATHERINE.*)* Your hair is lovely. Maria did a very nice job.

CATHERINE: Shall I put on the grey dress?

LAVINIA: Sage green, dear.

CATHERINE: It looked grey.

LAVINIA: This color is just as nice on you.

CATHERINE: I swear it was the exact red in that photograph.

LAVINIA: Indoor lighting.

CATHERINE: This is indoor lighting! What shall I do?

LAVINIA: Nothing, dear. It will be fine.

CATHERINE: You say that about everything!

LAVINIA: That's because it's true.

CATHERINE: Everything isn't fine!

LAVINIA: *(About life, not the dress color)* If you look at it close enough, it is.
So let's just concentrate on the problem at hand.

CATHERINE: Oh, you do think this dress is a problem. You do.

LAVINIA: No, I didn't say that.

CATHERINE: You did. And it is. I chose this particular red because of that picture of Father and Mother, he's wearing that tie…it looked like the same red.

LAVINIA: We should have taken it with us.

CATHERINE: The photograph? Oh no.

LAVINIA: Why didn't we?

CATHERINE: Because it's their wedding picture. And it's always been by Mother's bed. It's almost sacrilegious to move it.

LAVINIA: It's a bit of a shrine she has there.

CATHERINE: Aunt Liv, you wore black for a decade. Sorry, that wasn't nice what I said.

LAVINIA: True.

CATHERINE: That it wasn't nice? I'm sorry. I'm sorry.

LAVINIA: No, Catherine. It's true I stayed in mourning for too many years. Now, we loved this dress in the store. And it's beautiful.

CATHERINE: Whatever it is, my mother is going to hate it.

LAVINIA: You don't know that.

CATHERINE: Oh yes, I do.

(ELEANOR *enters from upstairs, in her dress for the party*)

ELEANOR: Arthur is always on time! We are late— (*Stops when she sees* CATHERINE) Oh my god.

CATHERINE: You look so beautiful, Mother.

(ELEANOR *comes down the stairs*)

LAVINIA: Her hair is nice.

CATHERINE: Maria did my hair.

(MARIA *appears.*)

ELEANOR: Satisfactory job, Maria.

(MARIA *exits.*)

CATHERINE: I had these shoes.

ELEANOR: I told you to get pumps.

CATHERINE: Aunt Lavinia helped me—

LAVINIA: They show off her ankles, in a nice way, that's not too provocative.

ELEANOR: How can an ankle be provocative? Are you living In the last century, Lavinia? Really. I told you to get her pumps because they show off the ankle *and* the arch. She has nicely-shaped feet. Let's accentuate the positive.

CATHERINE: Would the grey dress be better?

ELEANOR: There's no time to change without messing up your hair and, no, the sage green, *haute couture* dress is moot, at this point. And you have no shoes. You were supposed to be shopping for shoes to go with that dress. And these scarlet heels will not go with a sage green dress. Do you have hose on?

CATHERINE: Of course, Mother.

ELEANOR: And that new girdle? *(Feels for it and finds it)* Throw your shoulders back, Catherine. It moves the breasts up to prominence.

(From the street, the sound of a taxicab door shutting)

ELEANOR: Oh God, people are arriving! Maria!

CATHERINE: Let me check on the canapés.

ELEANOR: I checked. Everything is fine. I finally found a caterer that can do good work.

CATHERINE: Thank you, Mother. I did the canapés! I'll check on them. *(She exits into the kitchen.)*

ELEANOR: What?

(The doorbell rings. MARIA enters to answer it)

ELEANOR: Lavinia! This party is to present Catherine to Arthur's cousin. Get her out of the kitchen! Arthur's cousin isn't coming to meet a kitchen maid!

(MARIA *re-enters with* ARTHUR TOWNSEND, *a nattyily-dressed lawyer-accountant,* ARTHUR *is* ELEANOR's *age and an old friend)*

ARTHUR: Ellie!! How are you!!! Where are the martinis?

ELEANOR: Where is your cousin?

ARTHUR: *(Asking about the martinis)* Maria?

MARIA: The bar has been moved to the garden, Mr Townsend. *(She exits.)*

ELEANOR: Where is your cousin?

ARTHUR: He insisted on buying some liqueur. As a *present* to the house. He's very proper. Well-brought up. Lived in Europe, you know.

ELEANOR: And how is he related to you?

ARTHUR: My father's brother who lived in Antibes. Younger brother.

ELEANOR: And that is—

(MARIA *re-enters with icebucket which she puts down and then re-exits.* ELEANOR *and* ARTHUR *continue their conversation)*

ARTHUR: The French Riviera.

ELEANOR: So he's French?

ARTHUR: No no no no. He is a Townsend. He was educated in America. He has no accent.

ELEANOR: What American schools? Where?

ARTHUR: Stuyvescent.

ELEANOR: That's a public high school.

ARTHUR: It's a very difficult school to get into.

ELEANOR: Yes, I know. I know. But why not a private school? Your family has the money.

ARTHUR: He's very bright.

ELEANOR: And they're dummies at Choate? Andover? Exeter?

ARTHUR: He was at Andover. He missed the city.

ELEANOR: Why didn't he go to college?

ARTHUR: He...missed...France.

ELEANOR: He sounds difficult or diffident, anyway.

ARTHUR: Give him a chance, Eleanor. Now where's my martini?
And where is Catherine?

ELEANOR: In the kitchen seeing to the canapés!
I'll make you a martini. Secret Stash? Remember?
(Speaks as she makes two martinis and waves the empty bottle of Vermouth over the mix as she is talking) What am I to do, Arthur? She insists on acting like the help Instead of coming into her own and measuring up to her inheritance. To think my family money will be in the hands of some girl who could very easily be mistaken for someone who should use the service entrance to her own home!

(ELEANOR hands ARTHUR his martini.)

ELEANOR: I hope that's enough *Vermouth.*

ARTHUR: *(Tastes it)* Perfect.

ELEANOR: Who else is coming?

ARTHUR: Some young people. But Morris is the one I'd hoped you'd be interested in.

ELEANOR: Where is he? Is he afraid to meet me?

ARTHUR: Although you can be a little intimidating, sometimes, Eleanor, he's not afraid to meet you. He's accomplished in his own right. He studied to be a musician. And he's been all over the world.

ELEANOR: He "studied"?? Where is the statement that "he finished a degree in something"?

ARTHUR: The money ran out for his education. And I offered to pay, but Morris had left for Paris by then.

ELEANOR: Who does he think he is? Hemingway?

ARTHUR: He went to *Paris*, on his own. To learn about life, to better himself.

ELEANOR: To "better" himself? He's a Townsend.

ARTHUR: To be educated, Eleanor.

ELEANOR: Educated? In what? Drinking wine on the Mouffetard? Does he have a profession? Some gainful employment? Is he broke? Is that what's you're saying to me? You brought me a penniless, professionless young man as a prospect for Catherine.

ARTHUR: He is a Townsend, as you pointed out. And he's damned attractive. And Catherine—well, you know I love her as if she were my own daughter— we've talked about this, Ellie—what does Shakespeare say about a woman who's not classically pretty? She's "not for all markets."

ELEANOR: Her father was so handsome. He looked like Cary Grant. Wasn't he handsome, Arthur?

ARTHUR: Yes. Yes, he was.

ELEANOR: Catherine is darker than her father. And her body—she's starting to look like one of those women you see, you know, with several children, in areas of the city—

ARTHUR: Harlem.

ELEANOR: She's not that dark. For heaven's sake, Arthur. Those are Negroes. She's just Spanish—

ARTHUR: *Spanish* Harlem, then?

CATHERINE: *(Entering, with a tray)* Canapés?

ARTHUR: Catherine!

ELEANOR: Oh, for heavens sake, Catherine. Put down that tray!

CATHERINE: Excuse me, Mother. It's not meant to rest— it's for serving. You don't just put it down somewhere for people to pick at.

(Doorbell rings. MARIA *enters to answer it)*

ELEANOR: Maria, take the tray!

*(*MARIA *is confused.* CATHERINE *exits with the tray.* MARIA *exits to answer the door)*

MORRIS: *(Offstage)* Oh. You must be Maria. Hello.

ELEANOR: *(Noting* MORRIS's *questionable behavior)* He speaks to staff, Arthur.

*(*MORRIS TOWNSEND *enters with* MARIA, *who exits.* MORRIS *is well-dressed, elegant, even. He is of some white and African heritage. He carries a bottle of Courvoisier which he gives to* ELEANOR*)*

MORRIS: Hello. I am Morris Townsend. And you must be the famous Dr Eleanor Sloper.

ELEANOR: Arthur?

ARTHUR: Morris knows all about your professional achievements. And those of Miguel. And he knows about your service, as a couple, in the war.

MORRIS: World War Two. Not Korea. A real war. I was a baby, In France, when the Germans were there. I don't remember, of course, but I know my mother suffered some terrible…things. She loved the Americans and made certain I was raised in this country.

ARTHUR: His father's country.

ELEANOR: Arthur—

MORRIS: *(About some object d'art in the room)* Look at this. Twelfth Century? There's something like this at the Cluny. Or the Courtald, in London.

ARTHUR: Morris has been to London.

MORRIS: It's an easy jaunt from Calais on the boat-train. This house is so beautiful! So many beautiful things.

ELEANOR: Arthur, may I—

MORRIS: Dr Sloper, I'm sorry. I should be focusing on you. And your daughter? Catherine? You look much too young to have a daughter who is eighteen, is it?

ELEANOR: Thank you.

MORRIS: I'm humbled, frankly, by your accomplishments and your attractiveness. Arthur talks about you all the time.

ARTHUR: I've been trying to get Eleanor to marry me, but she refuses. I'm not highly-accomplished, just a lawyer.

ELEANOR: You never ask me seriously, Arthur.

ARTHUR: How's that martini coming?

ELEANOR: We're out of Vermouth.

MORRIS: Shall I go out and get some? I do know this neighborhood. I spent a few years around here, before being moved to the East Side, to be near my school.

ARTHUR: Very respectable, Ellie. Very respectable. On *this* side of Houston.

MORRIS: What are you saying, Arthur? I am a member of your esteemed family. I apologize for my cousin's rudeness, Madame.

ELEANOR: No need to apologize for Mr Townsend, Mr Townsend. I'm sure he has my best Interests at heart. *(To* ARTHUR*)* If I could speak to you, Arthur, alone, for a moment.

MORRIS: Of course. I'll just go…to the kitchen?

ELEANOR: No. To the garden.

MORRIS: You have a garden?

ARTHUR: There's no need for Morris to go anywhere. Anything you have to say about him, I'd like him to hear directly. Stay, Morris.

(Beat)

ELEANOR: When one has an eligible daughter who will inherit a fortune, one has to be—

MORRIS: —careful. I understand—

ELEANOR: —Vigilant. I'm a physician, so I can judge people quickly and correctly. It's a necessary skill.

MORRIS: And what do you see, Dr Sloper, when you look at *me*?

(Beat. Is she going to mention his complexion?)

ELEANOR: A charmer. You are a charmer, Morris Townsend.

(MARIA enters and places ashtrays.)

MORRIS: I don't smoke.

ELEANOR: We are expecting *others*, aren't we, Arthur? It is a party?

ARTHUR: Oh, yes. Of course.

ELEANOR: Martini for you, Morris?

MORRIS: I prefer wine.

ELEANOR: In the garden.

MORRIS: Which way….

ELEANOR: Maria? Show Mr Townsend to the garden, will you?

(MARIA is confused.)

ELEANOR: The younger Mr Townsend. And keep him out of the kitchen.

(MARIA *exits with* MORRIS.)

ARTHUR: I know how *you* are, Eleanor. But I have to have some Vermouth.

ELEANOR: Arthur, he is a Negro.

ARTHUR: His mother is from French Algeria.

ELEANOR: What are they there? Negro or white?

ARTHUR: Eleanor, sometimes your ignorance…it's not becoming; it's not worthy of you.

ELEANOR: Are they even Christian?

ARTHUR: His mother was Catholic.

ELEANOR: Catholic. Well, at least, he's not Jewish.

ARTHUR: He could be Jewish. He has that hair they have.

ELEANOR: What kind of hair?

ARTHUR: The kind of hair you can stick a pencil in and it doesn't move.

ELEANOR: You are making fun of me.

ARTHUR: Well, what am I supposed to do, Eleanor? You were so defensive about the least mention of Miguel's…color. There are women in the Hamptons who bake out in the sun to get that color. All right, Morris is less than one half Negroid. His mother was a mulatto.

ELEANOR: Look, I don't care about the percentages. The point is, he is colored. He is a colored person.

ARTHUR: And so is Catherine.

ELEANOR: Catherine is half…Spanish, that's all.

ARTHUR: Morris is half French.

ELEANOR: It's not the same, Arthur! The French are white! Wait—

ARTHUR: Right. Then Morris might not accept Catherine. Because she is brown.

ELEANOR: But…

ARTHUR: Yes?

ELEANOR: You are trying to perpetrate something here.

ARTHUR: Catherine is like my daughter.

ELEANOR: Then why are you trying to marry her to—

ARTHUR: What?

ELEANOR: Society will never accept them!

ARTHUR: "Society" loved Miguel.

ELEANOR: He was from Harvard! He was brilliant! He was like—I don't know—Cesar Romero!

ARTHUR: Cesar Romero is queer.

ELEANOR: What?

ARTHUR: Cesar Romero is homosexual.

ELEANOR: What? Why are we talking about Cesar Romero?

ARTHUR: You brought him up.

ELEANOR: What are you saying? My Miguel was not, NOT, one of those—

ARTHUR: Of course, he wasn't, Eleanor. And neither is Morris.

ELEANOR: Well, of course, Morris isn't homosexual. That would be ridiculous.

ARTHUR: So everything is fine. I like Morris. He has the best qualities of the family. You will see that. Now where is Catherine?

ELEANOR: Fine? Catherine is in the kitchen acting like a servant. And then you bring, as a serious suitor, some—

ARTHUR: Negro?

ELEANOR: Not a "negro" —he's clearly not that. He's... If his hair were straighter...

ARTHUR: He'd "pass"?

ELEANOR: In this entire city, there isn't one white man available to marry Catherine?

ARTHUR: You've tried your way. And spent quite a bit of money on wardrobe, cotillions, with no results. There was that pimply-faced young scion, distant relative of the Vanderbilts, and that wild boy, what was his name, who kept monkeys, and the fake count, and, of course, one of the Kennedys they were trying to get rid of. There are plenty of older prospects. Of course, they all want blondes.

ARTHUR: He is a Townsend, as you pointed out. And he's damned attractive.

ELEANOR: You keep saying that, Arthur. Perhaps *you* should marry him.

(LAVINIA *leads* CATHERINE *into the room.* CATHERINE *has the tray.* LAVINIA *is clearly backing up her niece's culinary talents)*

CATHERINE: Hello, Arthur. Canapés?

ELEANOR: Catherine, put down that tray.

CATHERINE: Sorry, Mother. But see how beautiful they are? These are Cucumber Cream Canapés. I made the puff pastry myself yesterday. And these are white fish—

ELEANOR: Put the tray down, Catherine!

MORRIS: *(Entering)* I'd like one.

(CATHERINE *turns to see* MORRIS. *She freezes.*)

MORRIS: I'll take the tray, shall I?

(He takes the tray from her.)

ARTHUR: Morris, this is Catherine Sloper, Eleanor's, that is to say, Dr Sloper's daughter.

MORRIS: *(Taking* CATHERINE's *hand)* En chanté.

(CATHERINE *is frozen.* MORRIS *hands the tray to* ARTHUR, *then takes one of the canapés, eats it.)*

This is very good. Oh, I'm sorry, let me offer you one. After all, you made them.

CATHERINE: I've had some. Quite a lot. I'm sort of sick of them now.

ARTHUR: What are they?

CATHERINE: Cucumber cream In pastry shells. I made them from scratch. Well, God made the cucumber, of course. And the dairy. With the cow's help. But the puff pastry—well, I folded it so many times—I don't know how many layers. I just kept spreading the butter and folding the dough and putting it back In the frig, spreading the butter and folding the dough and putting it back In the frig, spreading the butter and folding the dough and putting it back In the frig, because the butter, can't get too melted or the whole thing will just turn to mush and only good for not very good pie dough.

MORRIS: You made the canapés?

CATHERINE: To save money. And homemade tastes the best, anyway.

ELEANOR: Catherine!

CATHERINE: I'm so sorry, Mother.

ELEANOR: We don't need to save money, Mr Townsend.

ARTHUR: As your financial advisor, I think it's always commendable to save money.

ELEANOR: May we stop talking about money thank you.

MORRIS: Well, these canapés are certainly good. And made with such beautiful hands.

CATHERINE: Oh. Okay.

ELEANOR: I'd like to speak to my daughter alone. Mr Townsend.

ARTHUR: Eleanor...

MORRIS: Of course. *(He bows slightly—perfect manners.)*

ELEANOR: Oh, and this is my sister, Lavinia. Good-bye, everyone.

(ARTHUR, MORRIS and LAVINIA exit to the garden, LAVINIA shooting her sister a parting, critical glance.)

CATHERINE: Mother, may I start over, please? I know I shouldn't have fussed over the canapés. "Spreading the butter and folding the dough and putting it in the frig"—I must have said that about eighty times. I just get so—

ELEANOR: Catherine. This dress! Oh, it doesn't matter.

CATHERINE: I know it's off the rack or whatever that is you hate. But this color of red—

ELEANOR: —looks cheap!! You look like a street-walker!! Oh, what difference does it make?

CATHERINE: I do not look like a streetwalker, Mother.

ELEANOR: We become what we look like. Everything is from the outside in. That is what makes people whomever they are. And that's why you must look...

CATHERINE: What, Mother. Tell me what to do and I'll do it.

ELEANOR: Clearly, you won't. Case In point. There is a beautiful dress upstairs, In a beautiful color. But you had to go shopping and get this...thing you're wearing.

CATHERINE: I'll go upstairs and change.

ELEANOR: No. I'm going to go upstairs. I'll be upstairs.

CATHERINE: Are you not feeling well, Mother? Is it one of your headaches?

ELEANOR: Let's say it is.

ARTHUR: *(Entering)* Knock, knock.

ELEANOR: Not now!

ARTHUR: *(He's playing a child's game with* CATHERINE, *something they played when she was little)* KNOCK. KNOCK.

CATHERINE: Who's there?

ARTHUR: Honey Bee.

CATHERINE: Honey Bee who?

ARTHUR: Honey *be* a dear and get me another martini. You know how to make them the best, Catherine.

*(*MORRIS *enters,* ELEANOR *heads for the stairs)*

ARTHUR: Ellie! Where are you going?

MORRIS: Never ask a beautiful woman where she is going, Uncle Arthur. And in such a stunning gown.

(Takes ELEANOR's *hand an kisses it. She is stopped by the formality and then softened by his charm.* MORRIS *dances* ELEANOR *around slowly—he's used to charming women. There is a moment of possible sexual attraction between them but* ELEANOR *pulls away)*

CATHERINE: Be careful. Mother has a headache.

MORRIS: Oh. Sorry.

ARTHUR: Beautiful dress, Catherine.

ELEANOR: Men are so stupid.

Except for Miguel.

ARTHUR: Can you imagine how tired if am of hearing about the the perfection of Miguel? If he were so perfect, Ellie, why didn't you keep his name? Too *foreign* for you? Not Pilgrim, not Dutch. "Artecona." Cathy, you would have been Catherine Artecona. It's a beautiful name.

ELEANOR: You're getting unpleasant, Arthur. No more martinis.

ARTHUR: I'll just go to straight gin, thank you.

ELEANOR: Oh, that's all we drink around here, you know that.

MORRIS: *(Rescuing* CATHERINE*)* Shall we go to the garden? Excuse us?

(CATHERINE *goes with* MORRIS *to the garden.*)

ELEANOR: Make *me* another martini, immediately, Arthur! And add some cynanide to yours!

ARTHUR: I don't understand.

ELEANOR: What prospects does he have?

ARTHUR: He is a member of my family.

ELEANOR: Which part, Arthur? You and I have talked about the various "branches" of your old, old family. Which branch is Morris from? Anywhere near the original Charter Oak that produced you and all your family prestige? Is he even part of the bloodline? At all?

ARTHUR: You're getting tipsy, Eleanor.

ELEANOR: And I plan to get more so. That red dress she's wearing. She's trying to match the color of her father's tie in that photo. Of course, he was out of uniform. But they wouldn't touch *him*. They knew

what they had. Their most brilliant surgeon, from
Harvard, marrying into the Slopers, a good, strong,
New York City family of Pilgrim—yes, Pilgrim you
were right, Arthur—stock. His young, blonde bride,
also a brilliant medical student, also ready to help
save the world from the Nazis. The two of us. And I so
adored him. And I got pregnant which meant I lost my
commission, so I had to come home to have our baby,
to this house. And one day, two soldiers came to the
door, that very door and I wasn't going to let them in.
But Maria, no, not Maria, what was her name? Elena.
Helena. Helena opened the door, that very door out
there. And they came in and killed me. They killed me,
Arthur.

ARTHUR: I know, Ellie.

ELEANOR: And now his daughter, dressed like that
whore In that opera who kills her boyfriend, you know
it! That Spanish harlot—

ARTHUR: Carmen.

ELEANOR: Carmen! That's right. Carmen. She's dressed
like Carmen and she's in the garden with your ne'er-
do-well relative of—of questionable lineage, who is not
white and they're probably going to fall In love, or she
will fall In love with him because she's never known
anything like that, and they'll want to marry.

ARTHUR: Eleanor—

ELEANOR: I will never forgive you for this!

ARTHUR: What?

ELEANOR: Pawning off this dark horse in your family—

ARTHUR: Ellie—maybe some coffee—

(A taxicab arrives and we hear voices from the street)

ELEANOR: Oh, good. Other "young people" are
arriving!! Let's have a cotillion right here. None of

the others did any good. Catherine stood like a stick through every single one, too terrified to accept any of those strong-armed boys who at least pretended to want to dance with her. And now it's all moot. Like the sage green dress. Moot. Because all is lost.

(CATHERINE *enters, running and exits upstairs.* LAVINIA *enters, looking for* CATHERINE)

LAVINIA: Where is she?

ELEANOR: She just went upstairs.

LAVINIA: What did you say to her? *(Not waiting for an answer. She exits up the stairs.)*

(Doorbell rings. MARIA *enters to answer it, exiting to the front door)*

ELEANOR: More company! Well, so far, it's been a wonderful party!

*(*MORRIS *enters from the kitchen)*

ARTHUR: *(To* MORRIS*)* What did you do?

MORRIS: Nothing. As soon as we were alone, I couldn't get her to talk.

ELEANOR: *(To* MORRIS*)* I expected more from you, Mr Townsend. A man of the world such as yourself being cowed by a young, naïve girl. But I am relieved.

MORRIS: I'm going. Don't worry, Dr Sloper. It's clear you don't approve of me. I'll take the service exit. I'll get a cab, Arthur. Good night.

*(*MORRIS *exits towards the kitchen to leave).*

ARTHUR: Eleanor. Really. You can be soooo—

ELEANOR: Wanting the best for my only child?

MARIA: *(Re-entering)* Dr Sloper—there are a lot of young people out here and a very angry cab driver…. Evidently, they forgot to bring anything smaller than a fifty dollar bill.

ELEANOR: I believe it is *your* party now, Arthur.

ARTHUR: I'll take care of it. Thanks, Maria. *(He downs the last of his martini and heads for the door.)*

ELEANOR: *(Suddenly missing her husband)* Miguel. Where are you? Dammit!

Oh, my headache's back. I could just throw up.

(End of Scene One)

Scene Two

(Later that night. MARIA is cleaning up the mess from the party. CATHERINE enters wearing pajamas and a robe and begins to also clean up glasses, etc.)

MARIA: Miss Catherine—

CATHERINE: Were all my canapés eaten?

MARIA: Everything was eaten, Miss.
And drunk. Or "drank" is probably correct.

CATHERINE: Either. Or either. How long did it go on— the party?

MARIA: Once the people arrived in the cab. Well, they brought their own party. And Mr Townsend, Mr Arthur Townsend, seemed to enjoy them. Your mother stayed up for a while. And then, when everything was eaten and drank, everybody went home.

(Doorbell rings. MARIA looks to CATHERINE and CATHERINE nods—MARIA answers. MORRIS enters)

MORRIS: Catherine—

CATHERINE: Oh no. Oh no!!

(CATHERINE starts to run upstairs. MORRIS grabs her by the arm. They are frozen there.)

MARIA: Miss?

MORRIS: *(To* CATHERINE, *letting go of her arm)* Go if you want to. Upstairs. Are you afraid of me? Not cool, Miss Catherine. Fear of men. It's not cool. You left me in the garden.

CATHERINE: *(To* MARIA*)* You can go, Maria. It's all right.

*(*MARIA *exits.)*

MORRIS: I'm going to make you talk to me. Come over here and sit down. Come on. Come on... Shall I call Maria back? Would you be more comfortable?

*(*CATHERINE *finds a place to sit and sits)*

CATHERINE: I'm in my pajamas.

MORRIS: They have doggies on them.

CATHERINE: Yes.

MORRIS: What kind of dogs are they?

CATHERINE: *(Not looking to see)* It's Lady and the Tramp.

MORRIS: That would be from the movie?

CATHERINE: Yes.

MORRIS: You liked this movie.

CATHERINE: Oh, yeah. I loved it. Did you like it?

MORRIS: I didn't see it.

CATHERINE: How old are you?

MORRIS: I'm twenty-six. *(Pause)* But I heard it was really...really...cute. Like you.

CATHERINE: These pajamas are really old, really, really old. Mother hates them. She wouldn't even let me take them to Vassar. I've had them since I was a kid. I know I am nineteen. But I still love Lady and the Tramp. And I haven't gotten much taller since I was wearing these new. So they were ski pajamas? But I wore holes in the knees. So I cut off the legs and hemmed them and now they're shorts. And they are frayed but I don't care I hide them and put them on after Mother has gone to bed, because Mother would be so angry and I just hate making her angry. It almost makes me sick. So I need to go because if she caught me down here, she would be so angry and that look she gives me…

MORRIS: But all we're doing is talking, Catherine.

CATHERINE: But I'm not dressed! My hair isn't done! I don't have any make-up—oh no, I forgot to take it off. It's probably smeared.

MORRIS: You look fine.

(Beat)

CATHERINE: Mother doesn't like you.

MORRIS: I know.

CATHERINE: You want to talk to her?

MORRIS: No!

CATHERINE: Don't you want to make up with her?

MORRIS: Maybe someday. I don't think she thinks I'm worthy…

CATHERINE: Of what?

MORRIS: Of you.

CATHERINE: What?

MORRIS: Don't you know I was brought here to meet you?

CATHERINE: Okay. Yes.

MORRIS: You're blushing.

CATHERINE: I'm upset.

MORRIS: Is that why you're blushing?

CATHERINE: I know I'm a disappointment to her. I've tried to be the kind of daughter she wants. I don't know how to do it. Right now—if she came down here—!!

MORRIS: I would protect you.

CATHERINE: How?

MORRIS: I would pretend you were trying to throw me out and I wouldn't leave.

CATHERINE: Right. Because that would make her think—what?

MORRIS: That you were being a proper young lady.

CATHERINE: And not—

MORRIS: A beautiful young woman receiving a man.

CATHERINE: Oh.

MORRIS: In her pajamas.

CATHERINE: "A beautiful young woman—"

MORRIS: That's you, Catherine.

CATHERINE: Oh.

MORRIS: Yes. Go on.

CATHERINE: "receivIng a man…"

MORRIS: "In her pajamas."

CATHERINE: That sounds like you're in my pajamas.

MORRIS: Maybe I'd like to be.

CATHERINE: But you'd look silly.

MORRIS: In your pajamas?

CATHERINE: Yes. First of all, they wouldn't fit you.

MORRIS: You are so…

CATHERINE: Not cool.

MORRIS: Sweet.

(MORRIS *caresses* CATHERINE*'s face with the back of his fingers.*)

CATHERINE: OooOHo. I should go.

MORRIS: Nooooo. Stayyyy.
This house is so beautiful. Tell me about it.

CATHERINE: Okay. Mother decorated it for Father, but he never got to see it.

MORRIS: I'm sorry. So you never met him?

CATHERINE: No.
Here's a picture of him. He was very handsome.

MORRIS: You have his eyes.

CATHERINE: Do I, really?

MORRIS: What does you mother say about the resemblance?

CATHERINE: She says those looks are better on a man. Do I look manly?

MORRIS: No, Cathy. No.

CATHERINE: I hope not.

MORRIS: No one would ever think you're anything but the cutest, prettiest little girl in the world. And… (*He doesn't say what he's thinking which is "sexy".*)

CATHERINE: Thank you.

MORRIS: There's a carpet that's Persian.

CATHERINE: You mean the rug?

MORRIS: I spent some time In Morocco. Saw these in the markets.

CATHERINE: Isn't Morocco in Africa?

MORRIS: Not that far from Paris. Europe is quite small. America is huge. I want to go across country someday.

To California. I've been taking a course at Columbia. In the history of the Americas.

CATHERINE: What are "the Americas?"

MORRIS: This land we're on. It's a continent.

CATHERINE: I-I studied French poetry of the 15th century.

MORRIS: Why?

CATHERINE: *(A transgression and a confidence)* Mother had no interest in it and then I could have something of my own. I haven't always stayed in this house, you know. I've been to different schools. In other places.

MORRIS: Where?

CATHERINE: Connecticut. Miss Porter's.

MORRIS: I was at Andover for a year. But I left.

CATHERINE: Why? You didn't like Boston?

MORRIS: I wasn't in Boston. Andover is in a town that's just a bunch of houses. No city, anywhere. I was a project, you know. Being colored. And I was an athlete, too. But I was never accepted. And they prayed funny. You had to go to chapel and you sat in these pews and us boys, we had to fold ourselves in half so that our heads were between our knees and our arms were at our sides. And that's how we prayed.

CATHERINE: Why?

MORRIS: We didn't dare ask.

CATHERINE: Mother pulled me out of Miss Porter's because they didn't teach enough science. She was trying to find schools that taught that. But at Vassar, I wouldn't kill my rat. It's not right that you should kill any animal just to learn something. And it's something somebody already learned and then they killed their rat. And somebody before that killed a rat to learn something else. And then we have all these dead rats. And for what?

MORRIS: Do you like rats?

CATHERINE: No. But that doesn't mean they should just be killed.

MORRIS: They're not good in the house. Some people in this very city have rats in their apartments.

CATHERINE: No! That's just wrong.

MORRIS: And they bite babies.

CATHERINE: Oh no. My lab rat didn't bite at all. She was pretty and white with pink where she didn't have hair.

(Sound from upstairs. MARIA comes in, stares at them, they hide. After a beat, ELEANOR comes downstairs, in whatever she sleeps in, CATHERINE and MORRIS tuck themselves away and stay very still)

MARIA: *(To ELEANOR)* Oh, Madam. Can I get you anything?

ELEANOR: Headache. A different one. Those friends of Arthur's were fun, but I'm too old for that much carrying on.

MARIA: Yes, Madam.

ELEANOR: I was looking for… *(Sings Alka-Seltzer song)*
Plop, plop, fizz, fizz,
Oh, what a relief it is.
Miguel hated that song. He had good taste.

MARIA: I think there's some Coca-Cola.

(ELEANOR looks around the private stash bar.)

ELEANOR: Hair of the dog is best.

MARIA: *(Finds something In the private stash)* Here's a Coke, Madam.

ELEANOR: Oh, all right.

(ELEANOR *goes further into the living room, looking for gin, which threatens* MORRIS *and* CATHERINE *where they are hiding*)

ELEANOR: I give up. *(Exits upstairs with the Coke).*

MARIA: It's safe.

ELEANOR: *(From upstairs)* What did you say, Maria?

MARIA: Nothing, Madam. Just talking to myself.

ELEANOR: Carry on.

MARIA: Yes, Madam.

ELEANOR: *(Appearing)* Better yet, Maria. Go to bed. The housekeeper can finish this all up, whatever you're doing. There you go. Off to bed. Now, go! Turn out the lights.

(ELEANOR *waits while* MARIA *does this.)*

ELEANOR: I'm going to stand here until I see you go to your room.

(MARIA *exits to her room.* ELEANOR *exits, too).*

(Long beat)

MORRIS: Is it safe?

CATHERINE: Yes.

(CATHERINE *tries to get up.* MORRIS *holds her.)*

MORRIS: Not yet.

CATHERINE: But it's safe.

MORRIS: It's safe here. With me. Always.

CATHERINE: Is it?

MORRIS: Always.

CATHERINE: Morris?

(MORRIS *kisses* CATHERINE.)

CATHERINE: That was so nice.

MORRIS: I know.

(MORRIS *kisses* CATHERINE *again.)*

CATHERINE: Uhhhoooo.

(Lights go on. CATHERINE *and* MORRIS *freeze.* LAVINIA *enters from the kitchen.)*

LAVINIA: Cathy? I know you're down here. I took the back stairs to the kitchen and you're not there. I don't know what you're doing, but you need to come out. Oh god, if you've gone out tonight, I'll just…. Where would you go??

MORRIS: *(Standing)* She's here, Miss Penniman. And she's fine.

LAVINIA: Cathy!

(CATHERINE *stands, ready to be assassinated.)*

LAVINIA: Oh no! You're wearing those pajamas!!

MORRIS: They are her favorites. And she looks adorable in them.

LAVINIA: Take the back stairs to your room. If your mother saw you….

MORRIS: I'll see you tomorrow.

(MORRIS *squeezes her hand.* CATHERINE *exits into the kitchen.)*

MORRIS: Miss Penniman, I assure you, nothing improper—

LAVINIA: That's a disappointment, Mr Townsend. And I am *Mrs* Penniman. Listen to me. Save our girl. I had true love before he died. My sister had true love with her husband before he died. This house is haunted by dead loves. I don't want Catherine to be stuck here. But go for now. You have a friend in me, Mr—

MORRIS: Call me Morris.

LAVINIA: Morris. Good-night.

(MORRIS *kisses* LAVINIA*'s hand. She shows him out. She then touches the place on her hand where his lips were, gets an unexpected thrill.* MARIA *enters in her nightclothes, sleepy and pissed off.* LAVINIA *goes upstairs.* MARIA *goes to the door, locks it, says to the room)*

MARIA: Anybody else?

(MARIA *turns out the light and starts to exit to her room.* ELEANOR *enters at the top of the stairs, wearing her sleeping mask on top of her forehead and is speaking so loud because because her earplugs are in)*

ELEANOR: *(Loud)* I can't sleep because I keep hearing noises. Even with my earplugs. Is the door locked? Maria?

MARIA: Yes, ma'am.

ELEANOR: *(Loud)* See that you do!

(ELEANOR *exits to her bedroom.* MARIA *exits, then comes back in, exits)*

(End of Scene Two)

Scene Three

(A week later. Morning. LAVINIA *enters and checks the morning mail, finds an envelope [addressed to* CATHERINE *from* MORRIS*] and pockets it.* MARIA *enters from the kitchen.)*

MARIA: It's been a week since the party and Miss Catherine has gotten up and made some kind of pastry every day. Today it's sticky buns.

LAVINIA: If I miss any letters from Morris for Catherine, will you hide them, so I can give them to her without her mother knowing?

MARIA: Yes, Mrs Penniman.

LAVINIA: He has written to her once a day since the party. He wrote one on the Sunday, mailed it, another on the following Monday, mailed it, and kept doing that until she's got more than a week of notes I've managed to keep her mother from finding. Because I know my sister and Catherine would never know Morris had even contacted her. I've volunteered to leave this house, something I never do, and take her answers and mail them myself, but she refuses to write anything back. Young people's stubbornness stands between them and their own happiness so often— their stubbornness and their rashness. They're like pendulums, swinging back and forth. No wonder they act dizzy half the time.

MARIA: Yes, Mrs Penniman. Miss Catherine also made coffee.

(ELEANOR *appears, ready for the day.*)

ELEANOR: Lavinia, what are you babbling on about? Is that the mail? Give it to me.

(LAVINIA *hands her the mail.* CATHERINE *enters from upstairs. She has really made an effort to please her mother with her appearance)*

CATHERINE: *(To wherever her mother is)* Mother! Your coffee is ready. And I've made some cinnamon rolls. I made the dough yesterday so it could rise and—

ELEANOR: Coffee is enough. I don't want to put on any weight. I hope you're watching your weight, Catherine. Your side of the family…

CATHERINE: How are you feeling, Mother?

ELEANOR: Speak a little softer, please.

CATHERINE: Another headache?

ELEANOR: Where is Maria?

(MARIA *enters.)*

Why must Catherine make the breakfast?

CATHERINE: I enjoy it, Mother. Really. I like to be busy.

ELEANOR: Well, at least, serve it in French. Today is French. I want to think that your two years at Vassar came to something.

CATHERINE: *(In French)* Mother, I am so sorry. I just couldn't stay in that place. *(Entre nous, to save* LAVINIA *hearing any of it, and still speaking in French)* Living with Aunt Lavinia was so dreary. Poughkeepsie is so dreary. The winters, Mother.

ELEANOR: Alright, dear. I understand. Having Lavinia here has brought home to me that living with her has its challenges.

CATHERINE: *(In French)* She's lovely, but—

ELEANOR: No, she's not. She's a pain In the neck, Catherine. I do realize that. Listen. How about going to school here? Barnard?

CATHERINE: *(In French)* I told you I couldn't get in to Barnard, Mother.

ELEANOR: Columbia? That's a nice, quiet campus.

CATHERINE: *(In English)* Morris goes there.

ELEANOR: How do you know that?

LAVINIA: *(Entering)* I told her. He told me. Very good coffee, Cathy.

CATHERINE: *(For saving her from having to answer the question about* MORRIS*)* Thank you. So much.

ELEANOR: It's only coffee, for god's sake.

LAVINIA: Can you make a good cup of coffee, Ellie?

ELEANOR: I'm taking my mail with me to the office.

(ELEANOR *grabs her mail and begins opening one of the envelopes, reading it.* MARIA *appears with her briefcase and coat)*

CATHERINE: Have a good day, Mother.

ELEANOR: *(About the letter)* I've been invited to a conference. In Lyon. I'll need a translator. Maybe Arthur will know someone. *(To* CATHERINE*)* Try to become clever while I'm gone. There's a good girl.

(MARIA *helps* ELEANOR *with her coat and shuts the door behind* ELEANOR *when* ELEANOR *exits.)*

CATHERINE: I can't do anything that pleases her!

LAVINIA: You please me, Cathy. You always have.

MARIA: You're a very fine young lady, Miss.

(MARIA, *upset on* CATHERINE's *behalf, exits quickly.)*

CATHERINE: Ever since I came back from school, she hates me.

LAVINIA: Your mother doesn't hate you, dear. She's your mother.

CATHERINE: That's a tautology so it's false. See? I learned something.

LAVINIA: She's just worried about you, about your future.

CATHERINE: I'm not going to become a doctor.

LAVINIA: She knows that, dear.

CATHERINE: I just want to get married. Someday. And live here and have a family. And do the cooking. And we could do a lot better with buying fresh things, I can tell you that. But Mother doesn't want me to have anything to do with running the house. Maybe I'll become a nun! Get out of here. Study and teach. Or cook in the nunnery.

LAVINIA: Convent.

CATHERINE: I guess I'd have to become Catholic. My father was Catholic. Why wasn't I allowed to be Catholic?

LAVINIA: Because we're Protestants. And your father wasn't alive to insist.

CATHERINE: How can I become a nun if I'm not Catholic?

LAVINIA: You're just grasping at straws because you're frustrated with you mother.

CATHERINE: I know I am.
I just—I just can't feel my future. I know something else is supposed to happen. To me. My parents were in a war. And they knew they were saving the world. From Hitler. And other bad...dictators. I don't have anything. There are no Hitlers, anymore.

LAVINIA: There are the Russians.

CATHERINE: Well, yes.

LAVINIA: And atomic bombs out there to drop on us.

CATHERINE: What am I supposed to do about that? That isn't a war where I sign up to go serve. Mother and Daddy were doctors. Well, Mother still is. I know I'm a complete disappointment to her. I was born at the wrong time, Aunt Liv. I don't fit in.

(Doorbell. MARIA answers.)

MARIA: *(To person at door)* All right. Oh.

(Door shuts. MARIA enters with a two vases of flowers)

MARIA: There's another one out there. Leave the door open, the boy is coming back for his tip. Three vases of flowers!

(CATHERINE *goes to get the third vase of flowers left in the doorway, returns, reading the card*)

CATHERINE: This one is to "Dr Eleanor Sloper," from "M Townsend". That's Morris.

LAVINIA: This one is to me! How lovely! "Mrs Lavinia Penneman."

MARIA: This one must be for you, Miss Catherine.

(CATHERINE *trades vases with* MARIA)

MARIA: I'll take Dr Sloper's, shall I? And put it... where?

LAVINIA: *(Reading her card)* "From Morris Townsend." I got his full name.
What does yours say, Catherine?

CATHERINE: *(Reading it)* "To Lady, from Her Tramp."

LAVINIA: Cathy, you are blushing.

CATHERINE: No, I'm not. Oh, Aunt Liv! What am I going to do? Mother doesn't like him. He's been writing me every day.

LAVINIA: Oh, here's another one.

CATHERINE: *(Opens and reads it)* It's so frightening. She doesn't like him. The first man who has ever shown any interest in me—and my mother doesn't like him.

LAVINIA: I know, dear. It's not fair. You may have to defy her.

CATHERINE: What?

LAVINIA: You may have to go against her wishes.

CATHERINE: I can't stand it when she's angry with me.

LAVINIA: Then you must have a miserable life, sweetheart. Because she is angry with you all the time.

(CATHERINE *takes that in.*)

LAVINIA: That's not how mothers are supposed to act, Cathy. I don't know why my sister is so…hard. She was always so bright and did well in school and in unfeminine subjects, like biology and math. Other girls didn't like her. I barely liked her myself. Oh, that is a terrible admission. I think she feels alone. And a bit of an oddity. Her work has given her so much. But at a terrible cost.

CATHERINE: *(Real compassion)* I feel bad for her now.

LAVINIA: That's because you're capable of compassion. You have always been the sweetest, dearest young person. That is your father in you, Cathy. Even though you never knew him, he is in your heart. Why do you think your mother and he were serving in the field? Because *he* wanted to do something for the war effort. They both could have had practices on Park Avenue and never been in uniform. And that would have been fine with Eleanor.

CATHERINE: She did all of that for him?

LAVINIA: She had room for one person in her heart and that was your father.

CATHERINE: She didn't have room for me?

(LAVINIA notices MARIA who has been standing with ELEANOR's vase of flowers, listening to LAVINIA talk with CATHERINE)

MARIA: *(Trying to cover her purpose)* Excuse me. Where shall I put these?

LAVINIA: Put Dr Sloper's in the study. Mine shall stay In the kitchen. In that sunny window.

(MARIA exits to ELEANOR'S study. LAVINIA exits to the kitchen. MORRIS sneaks in the front door, grabs CATHERINE and gives her a big passionate kiss)

MORRIS: Cathy, I love you. You have to marry me. Or I shall…die. Please. I've done nothing but think about you since that night. Nothing. Nothing. Life has no meaning without you. I looked into your face, and I just knew—you were the one I've been looking for. All those places I've been, and you were right here.

LAVINIA: *(Offstage)* Cathy, is that the flower boy?

MORRIS: Cathy—

LAVINIA: *(Entering with her purse)* Here's money for a tip— *(Sees* MORRIS*)*

CATHERINE: Oh, Aunt Liv. Make him go away! Please! Please.

MORRIS: Cathy—

LAVINIA: Cathy, listen to me. You need to find what happiness you can. You will never have to worry about money. And most people do have to worry about that. That sweaty Richard Nixon on television has to worry about it. But his real treasure is that wife of his, and his daughters. That's what you need, dear, is someone to love you and whom you can love. Because when you don't have that anymore, the hole that is left can claim you. And you can become silly, like me, and live through others, or, hard, like your mother, and drink too much or just work until you drop. When will you stop being a little girl and live your life?

CATHERINE: Aunt Lavinia—

LAVINIA: I can't help you anymore. *(She exits.)*

CATHERINE: Morris?

MORRIS: Yes?

CATHERINE: Are you still there?

MORRIS: Yes.

CATHERINE: I thought you'd gone.

MORRIS: No.

CATHERINE: All your letters. They are full of so many words. I don't know you that way, that way you talk in those letters.

MORRIS: I worked on them.

CATHERINE: I have one here. *(About the letter)* Look at this.

MORRIS: *(Reads it)* Oh.

CATHERINE: My mother thinks you're a salesman, that you'll say whatever anybody wants to hear, particularly if those people are women.

MORRIS: Has your mother read these?

CATHERINE: She doesn't even know about them.

MORRIS: I meant all that. All that poetry and words...

CATHERINE: I want to believe you, but you need to say something I can believe.

MORRIS: I love you.

CATHERINE: But people say that all the time.

MORRIS: I love you...so much.

CATHERINE: At night, someone kisses me, tells me they love me, even loves me "so much", turns off the light, shuts the door, goes away, leaving me in my small bed. And I fall asleep, listening to my own breath and sometimes my heart. And then the light comes in and it's morning and I get up and live. And I know I'm young, but I'm tired of it, Morris. And "I love you." What does that mean? Aunt Lavinia loves me. My mother loves me, I guess.

MORRIS: Do you remember the first time or just any time when you notice something? Like spring. It's been winter and cold but there are days that are beautiful but it goes on so long that you forget something else is coming. So the first time you look up and see a green leaf and it's like you never saw one of those before. "What is that?" And then you remember, it's spring. And you know there will be more and more. That's how I feel when I see you.

I don't know if that's love—I'm just tryIng to tell you—

CATHERINE: Can we kiss again?

(MORRIS *kisses* CATHERINE, *she kisses back, then makes little fluttery hand movements, afraid to touch his face but wanting to.)*

CATHERINE: Can we do that? A lot?

MORRIS: I guarantee it.

(ELEANOR *re-enters, through the front door, she's come from the office.)*

ELEANOR: It is I, Maria. I forgot something— *(Sees* MORRIS*)* What are you doing here? Where's Cathy?

(CATHERINE *emerges.)*

ELEANOR: Why are you hiding? What's going on?

MORRIS: Nothing, Dr Sloper.

ELEANOR: Oh, you have no backbone. You are a schoolboy! Look at him, Catherine! Look at him, lying!

MORRIS: I have just asked Cathy to marry me.

ELEANOR: "Marry you?!" You were just strolling by and thought you'd stop in and propose marriage to this young girl you barely know?

(LAVINIA *enters.)*

ELEANOR: Lavinia, what's been going on?

CATHERINE: He does know me, Mother.

ELEANOR: "Know you?" You mean in the Biblical sense?

CATHERINE: No! How can you say that?

ELEANOR: Well, what am I to think? He meets you once, you run away to your room, and now he's back days later to ask you to marry him? Something must have happened In the meantime. People don't fall in love like that.

LAVINIA: That's not true, Eleanor. The Reverend and I—

ELEANOR: Oh, hold off on the romantic poppycock for now.

LAVINIA: And what about you and Miguel?

ELEANOR: Ohhhh, just stop! Lavinia! Please!

MORRIS: I love your daughter. Completely.

ELEANOR: I think you love this house. And that 12th century, whatever it is, expensive thing over there that has survived twenty years of household staff cleaning it.

(ELEANOR xs to the object and breaks it)

I saw you gasp. Cathy, did you see him gasp?

Well, my daughter is worth more to me than all of this. House, furnishings, money in the bank. And I'm not just giving her away to anyone.

CATHERINE: *(To her mother)* I mean that much to you?

ELEANOR: Of course you do. *(To MORRIS)* Now, I suggest you go.

CATHERINE: No! No, Mother. I want him to stay.

ELEANOR: I just broke a 12th century vase to show you what he's interested it. The money, Cathy. Your inheritance. Why do you insist on refusing to see the world as I see it? Where did you come from? How can you be my daughter? I know you are because they handed you to me. And you had all this black hair, like your father's. Look at me. This man is not for you.

CATHERINE: Who is for me, Mother?

ELEANOR: Someone else. Someone we'll find. We'll make more of an effort to find a nice young man. With a future. Who will *like* you, delight in your difference.

CATHERINE: My "difference"?

ELEANOR: From everyone else. Your exotic look. Your defended innocence. Your practical, almost rustic, interests.

(Beat)

CATHERINE: Morris?

MORRIS: Yes?

CATHERINE: I'll marry you.

MORRIS: Oh—
Cathy.

(Embrace. CATHERINE *is hyperventilating)*

MORRIS: Are you…all right?

(Phone rings. MARIA *goes to answer it.)*

ELEANOR: That's the hospital. I have to go back. *(Taking the phone from* MARIA*)* Yes. Yes. It's pre-eclampsia. I know. I'm on my way. *(Hangs up the phone)* Lavinia! *(She addresses* MORRIS.*)* I want you out of this house. Right now. Lavinia, see that he goes.

CATHERINE: No, Mother!

ELEANOR: *(To* MORRIS*)* If you have any sign of civilization in you, you will do as I ask.
Mr Townsend.

*(*CATHERINE *holds on to* MORRIS.*)*

CATHERINE: No, Mother!! I love him!

ELEANOR: *(To* MORRIS*)* Look at the pain you are causing her. You're tearing this family apart! Now go! Be a gentleman and get out of here!

LAVINIA: Eleanor!

ELEANOR: We're all upset. Morris needs to leave.

(Horn beep)

ELEANOR: That's my cab. All right.

(ELEANOR, undoing CATHERINE's hold on MORRIS, gently:)

ELEANOR: This is becoming a scene. And I hate scenes.
(Removing CATHERINE's arms from around his waist)

MORRIS: Cathy. I have to go. This isn't right.

CATHERINE: What isn't right?

MORRIS: This isn't the way we need to do it. We need to be respectable and get your mother's blessing.

CATHERINE: I don't care about respectability! All it's done is made me miserable! And alone!

LAVINIA: Cathy, come here. Come to me. Come on.

(MORRIS hands CATHERINE to LAVINIA.)

ELEANOR: There.
Now, Mr Townsend, I want to see you leave. And you are on your honor not to return.

(MORRIS exits.)

CATHERINE: I'm going with him, then.

ELEANOR: No, you're not. Lavinia?

(Cab honks again. ELEANOR exits)

LAVINIA: No, dear. Just wait. Your mother will calm down.

CATHERINE: Wait for what? She'll never agree. She hates me, Aunt Lavinia. She hates the way I look and what I'm interested in. Did you hear what she said? "Rustic Interests?" And I look "exotic?"

LAVINIA: She was upset. People say things—

CATHERINE: You're defending her! Why?

LAVINIA: Because I can't believe she means to be this mean.

CATHERINE: "Mean" —that's it. I'm her child. I'm alone, Aunt Lavinia.

LAVINIA: You will always have me.

CATHERINE: But I don't want to turn out the way you did. I want to be alive and live! I don't want to be a prisoner of this house. I don't want my life to be summed up by a bunch of needlework. Oh, I'm sorry. That was so hurtful, what I said.

LAVINIA: Stop apologizing! Stop it! I love you. You don't have to measure up or behave in a certain way. That's what love is.

CATHERINE: Then we're both alone.

LAVINIA: You look around. You'll see a lot of love like that. The person who is alone, is your mother. Now, don't start feelIng compassion for her right now. You have to fight for your life.

(MORRIS *enters from the back entrance to the house. He is beyond winded.*)

MORRIS: I ran.

(*Phone rings.* MARIA *answers, everyone freezes.*)

MARIA: Sloper residence.
Yes, we'll accept the charges.
Hello, Doctor.
No, ma'am. No visitors of any kind.
Miss Catherine is talking to Mrs Penniman. Do you want to speak to either of them?
Yes, ma'am.
(*She hangs up the phone*)
That was Dr Sloper. She never carries any change so she had to make a collect call. I accepted the charges. I hope that's all right.

LAVINIA: That was more than all right, Maria. And thank you.

(MARIA *curtsies and exits.*)

LAVINIA: I'll be…somewhere, if you need me. *(She exits.)*

CATHERINE: *(To* MORRIS*)* We're eloping

MORRIS: But…

CATHERINE: But, what?

MORRIS: I have no money.

CATHERINE: But I do. I have money from my father. And it's due me this year.

MORRIS: How much?

CATHERINE: Ten thousand dollars.

MORRIS: That's all?

CATHERINE: A year.

MORRIS: Oh.
But what about the house?

CATHERINE: That will come to us. Some day.

Morris, I have to know this. There's something I have to know. Do you love me? Or all of this?

MORRIS: I love you.

CATHERINE: Just me?

MORRIS: No one is "just me." I come with Arthur. You come with your mother and your Aunt Lavinia. I have a sister. And nieces and nephews.

CATHERINE: More family? I will love that so much. Morris. Just saying your name fills me with a feeling of such something, I don't know, but happy, a happy feeling. And I have missed that feeling. All my life.

(CATHERINE *leads* MORRIS *upstairs. They stop at the head of the stairs.)*

CATHERINE: I know you've been to France and places and that you're older. But I've never been...anywhere, Morris. Do you know what I'm...trying to say?

*(*MORRIS *hushes* CATHERINE, *then picks her up and they exit to her bedroom.)*

(End of Scene Three)

Scene Four

(That evening. ARTHUR *and* ELEANOR *in the living room, drinking cognac.)*

ARTHUR: So now do I get to know what happened to that object d'art on the sideboard in the hall?

ELEANOR: Oh, it fell off and broke. It was a reproduction. I never liked it, anyway.

ARTHUR: *(About the cognac they're drinking)* You have to admit, the boy has good taste.

ELEANOR: Okay. Good cognac. But how much taste is involved in reading a label?

ARTHUR: He had to know what he was reading. It could have been some rotgut American swill. "gen-you-wine Napoleanic old grand dad cognac made just last year."

ELEANOR: He can read French. So what? Isn't this where you say, "He's damned attractive."?

ARTHUR: Eleanor, I have acted as Catherine's father for most of her life and I would never do anything to hurt her. So why would you think—why won't you trust me after all these years?

ELEANOR: I didn't get where I am by trusting people. I couldn't trust men and I don't trust women. Now, this conference in France that I was invited to a few weeks ago, I'm going to it. It's important. I'm giving a paper, at their request, on birth control *pills*. They are taken every day, orally. Searle has developed them. The combination of two hormones prevent pregnancy.

ARTHUR: What?

ELEANOR: I'm going to that conference in France. I've decided.

ARTHUR: Yes.

ELEANOR: It's important.

ARTHUR: Well, of course it's important. Birth control. Pills?

ELEANOR: Yes.

ARTHUR: Do they work?

ELEANOR: Well, of course, they work, Arthur.

ARTHUR: You mean, a woman can take a pill and not get pregnant?

ELEANOR: Is this an issue you've had to deal with? Much?

ARTHUR: How does it work? Does she hold the pill between her knees?

ELEANOR: She takes the pill orally. She swallows it. With some water. Then the combination of two hormones, progestin and estrogen, in the pill, prevent ovulation.

(ARTHUR *has been made immobile by this much discussion of the female inner anatomy and* ELEANOR *takes this as lack of information on his part*)

ELEANOR: Ovulation is the descending of the egg into the uterus, ready to be—

ARTHUR: Stop.

ELEANOR: Fortunately, there are men in France, at least, who want to hear more. And more. And more.

ARTHUR: The French are a prurient race.

ELEANOR: Something occurred here today. I hate to spoil all this, fun chummery we've got going this evening, because sometimes it is the only thing that I find tolerable about my private life, you, Arthur, our friendship, and it was nice eating alone, without Catherine and Lavinia, but they weren't really out somewhere, but in. In upstairs because Catherine is deeply upset and Lavinia is drawn to emotion like a fly to honey, but the Morris situation has become…it's on the brink of becoming…He has blinded her with romance, Arthur. And I fear she will say yes if he asks her to marry him.

ARTHUR: Would you give your consent?

ELEANOR: Let's see. He's unemployed and perhaps unemployable. He is broke and destined to stay that way *unless* he marries well. He loves this house.
And I assume my money. Now whom would be the perfect target for his amorous aspirations? *(She looks at* ARTHUR.*)*

ARTHUR: You?

ELEANOR: You say that with such ease. As if I am a prospect for anyone's amorous interest. *(Beat)* Isn't this where you ask me to marry you, Arthur? Seriously? *(Long beat)* Evidently not. Why is that, Arthur? Why do you only mention any interest in me when we are NOT alone?
Are you afraid I'll say "yes?"
Have you fallen asleep with your eyes open?
Men are such cowards. I don't know how they fight in wars.

ARTHUR: I—…

ELEANOR: Yes?

ARTHUR: Catherine will do what you tell her to do. She's a good girl.

ELEANOR: I can only hope you are right.

CATHERINE: *(Appearing at the top of the stairs)* Mother?

ARTHUR: There she is. *(Starts to sing The Miss America song)*
There she is….

CATHERINE: If you sing that stupid song, Arthur, I will fling myself down these stairs I'm not kidding.

ELEANOR: Catherine! I've always hated that song, but Arthur is our guest.

CATHERINE: No, he's not, Mother. He is a "member of the family," isn't that what you've always said. But what is our family? Three women? Is that all there is? Because—because— …I'm getting married, Mother. I'm marrying Morris.

ELEANOR: You are not marrying Morris Townsend. You are not!!

CATHERINE: I am. I'm of age. And I can marry whomever I want!! *(She's scared herself—this much defiance.)* Mother.

ELEANOR: Come down those stairs immediately!

(CATHERINE comes down the stairs)

ELEANOR: Now listen to me. Catherine. I don't know what's got into you, but marrying someone just to defy me is not a good beginning of a relationship. And no histrionics like we had earlier today.

CATHERINE: No, Mother.

ELEANOR: No, what?

CATHERINE: He said you would try to talk me out of it, but I'm not going to listen.

ELEANOR: "He." When did you talk to him? I threw him out of the house!

ARTHUR: Ellie! When?

ELEANOR: And there goes any fun for both of us for days now. Oh, can we just get past this?

ARTHUR: Where is Morris?

CATHERINE: She banned him from the house! He wanted to be here, but I said I would handle this on my own.

ELEANOR: You've never done anything on your own. Except leave Vassar. And I still blame Lavinia for not making you stick with it. Lavinia!! Where is she??

(LAVINIA *enters.*)

LAVINIA: Ellie, I think you need to listen to your daughter.

ELEANOR: Oh. I see. You're ganging up on me.

ARTHUR: I'll just—

ELEANOR: Arthur, sit down! You're not going anywhere.

(ARTHUR *obeys and finds a place to sit out of the action.*)

ELEANOR: What are you doing there? Go find your cousin!

(ARTHUR *rushes to the door and opens it to find* MORRIS. MORRIS *enters)*

ELEANOR: Oh! Here he is!! Were you listening at the door? Afraid to ring?

MORRIS: Cathy—

CATHERINE: I told her. We are getting married.

ELEANOR: Is that true? Morris?

MORRIS: I'm here to ask your permission to marry your daughter.

CATHERINE: I told you I could do this.

(MORRIS *"comforts"* CATHERINE *by shushing her.)*

MORRIS: I'm doing the right thing.

ELEANOR: No.

MORRIS: "No"?

ELEANOR: No.

CATHERINE: We're going to get married, either way, Mother. With or without your permission.

ELEANOR: Is that true, Morris?

MORRIS: We want your permission. Because that's the right way to do it. And your blessing.

ELEANOR: Let me talk to Morris alone. Arthur, stay here. Everyone else, leave.

(CATHERINE *gets an okay to leave from* MORRIS *and goes upstairs with* LAVINIA.)

ELEANOR: You certainly are an attractive man. I can see why my daughter has fallen for you. And "fallen" she has. Arthur? Drinks.

(ARTHUR *goes to fix drinks.)*

ELEANOR: She's a baby. And, no doubt, a virgin. Or, is she? Because that would be ignoble, Mr Townsend. I can read you like a book. You love fine things. You don't like to work. You're not a Lothario, but you've always had success with women.

(MORRIS *tries to speak,* ELEANOR *shuts his mouth with her fingers, then uses the opportunity to do something sensual.)*

ELEANOR: Women find you irresistible. I almost do.

MORRIS: Dr Sloper, you underestimate me.

ELEANOR: Do I? Well, let's see what you're made of. Here's the deal. Catherine inherits ten thousand dollars a year, starting on her birthday, which is in a month. If you marry her, you will have access to that money. However, if you marry her, you will never see a cent of my money, the Sloper money, which is— ...Arthur, how much am I worth?

ARTHUR: Two million and then there's the house.

ELEANOR: Two million you will never have, Morris, if you marry my daughter.

ARTHUR: The house goes to Cathy after your death, Eleanor.

ELEANOR: What's the maintenance and taxes on this house?

ARTHUR: About four thousand a year.

ELEANOR: So Cathy will have to spend some of that ten thousand on the house. Yearly.

MORRIS: You don't think I'm worthy of your daughter. And this property.

ELEANOR: Yes. That is true. Well said.

MORRIS: I have prospects.

ELEANOR: Does he, Arthur? Have prospects?

ARTHUR: I'm—I'm sure—

ELEANOR: Oh, what am I asking you for? You've never told me the truth.

ARTHUR: Oh, yes, I have, Ellie. I said, "I love you", once.

ELEANOR: I don't remember. Were we alone?

ARTHUR: Here's your drink.

ELEANOR: Thank you.

MORRIS: I know you don't know me well. And it seems like I don't have a future. But I know I will have one with Catherine. I do love her. And she makes me want to do things. Have dreams. Pursue some kind of life that isn't just getting a job in Arthur's firm.

ELEANOR: You should be so lucky.

ARTHUR: I'll hire him, Eleanor. If he marries Cathy. I know I could find something.

ELEANOR: Oh, now it comes out! This has been the plan all along! Marry this "problem relative" to my daughter and get our money because you don't have the manhood to marry me yourself!

ARTHUR: Eleanor!! That's enough!! That is not true!! Just because you're unhappy doesn't mean you have to poison everybody's else's life! I'm sorry Miguel died. You're not the only war widow. It's nearly twenty years. Enough of this—I'm leaving.

ELEANOR: No, you're not.

ARTHUR: Yes, I am. Good-bye, Morris. Let me know what happens. *(He starts to exit.)*

MORRIS: Arthur, wait!!

ELEANOR: If you think this changes anything, you are wrong. Marry my daughter and you'll be stuck with ten thousand a year and lots of bills.

MORRIS: I'm going to prove you wrong!

ARTHUR: I'm leaving, Morris. Come see me and maybe I can help.

MORRIS: Tell Cathy I'm coming right back for her.

(MORRIS exits after ARTHUR.)

ELEANOR: Everyone come down now!!

CATHERINE: Where's Morris?

ELEANOR: Gone.

CATHERINE: Gone?

MARIA: *(Entering)* Excuse me, Madam, I heard him say, "Tell Cathy I'm coming back for her."

LAVINIA: Is that right, Eleanor?

ELEANOR: Yes. That's what he said.

CATHERINE: Maria, go upstairs and finish packing my luggage.

(MARIA exits to do that.)

CATHERINE: You weren't going to tell me that he said he's coming back for me?

ELEANOR: Catherine, you're my daughter—

CATHERINE: Am I? Am I, Mother? What does that mean to you? "Your daughter." I have tried my entire life to please you. And I was found wanting. Always. Always, Mother. I had nannies who loved me more than you do. And when I got attached to one, you would fire her. Over some little thing she did. But another one would come. And she would like me. And I'd be afraid to show any sort of love for her because I knew that then she would be gone. So I learned to give my love in a general way, never too much to one person. So everybody loved me but I was still alone. You made certain of that.

ELEANOR: Because of you, I lost your father! The love of my life! I would have been there when he was wounded. I would have made certain that there was no chance of infection. I would have stayed by his side and nursed him, *doctored* him back to life.

CATHERINE: Why couldn't you be there?

ELEANOR: Because they kicked me out! When they found out I was pregnant! It didn't matter that we were married. They sent me home, like a schoolgirl who'd gotten knocked up by some grocery boy. So when your father got wounded in the field...I wasn't there, was I. He was doing his job as a doctor. But why he was put in such a vulnerable position, their chief of surgery. Why it wasn't some infantry scrub out there. But that was him. That was your father. Always thinking of other people first. Oh, Cathy. You're so much like him. Your have that giving spirit. Which I don't have.

CATHERINE: Oh, Mommy... *(She goes for an embrace.)* I don't want to hurt you. I don't.

ELEANOR: If you marry Morris Townsend, I will disinherit you. Promise me, you won't marry him. You owe me that, Catherine. I paid a terrible price for you. You owe me this promise: "I will not marry Morris Townsend". Say it. You owe me this. Say it.

CATHERINE: I will not say that. I will marry whoever I want to, Mother. Disinherit me. I don't care!!

ELEANOR: Whomever. And you are being so foolish!

CATHERINE: You cannot have my future. That belongs to me!

ELEANOR: I see you do have some of me in you. I can see it in your eyes. Well, we'll see who wins in the long run.

CATHERINE: "Wins," what? What will I "win?"

(MARIA appears at the top of the stairs with CATHERINE's luggage)

(LAVINIA gives CATHERINE a purse of money:)

LAVINIA: Arthur will see to it that your inheritance from your father is sent to whatever address you and Morris give us. Here is what cash I have and some jewelry you can pawn if you need more.

(MARIA piles the luggage up near the door.)

ELEANOR: Maria, you are dismissed.

MARIA: *(Thinks she's being fired)* Dismissed?

ELEANOR: Just for tonight.
You can go to bed.

LAVINIA: I'm staying up with Catherine. To say good-bye.
I think—

ELEANOR: I don't care what you think, Liv. Never have.
I'm going to bed. *(She climbs up the stairs.)*

CATHERINE: Mother? Mommy? Aren't you going to say Good-bye?

(ELEANOR pauses, doesn't look, and continues up the stairs and then exits to go to bed.)

CATHERINE: Aunt Liv—

LAVINIA: Courage, my darling. You're doing the right thing. *(Kisses her and exits upstairs)*

CATHERINE: I know I am.

(Long beat. CATHERINE goes to sit on her luggage)

(Light change. Night)

MARIA: *(Enters and looks at CATHERINE)* Would you like a chair?

(CATHERINE shakes her head "no")

CATHERINE: What is it, Maria?
What is it? Are you crying?
I'll miss you, too.

MARIA: That's not it.

CATHERINE: What do you mean?

MARIA: It's late, Miss Catherine.

CATHERINE: He's coming.

MARIA: I don't think he is.

CATHERINE: Don't say that!

MARIA: It's not my place. But I hate to see you sitting here. And you are so good.

CATHERINE: Leave me alone, Maria!

(MARIA *exits.* CATHERINE *waits.*)

END OF ACT ONE

ACT TWO

Scene One

(In the house. Some weeks? Months? Later. Maria *is looking out the front door.)*

Maria: Mrs Penneman?

Lavinia: Yes?

Maria: I think the cab is here.

Lavinia: Oh, good. I'm so glad Arthur could meet them. Oh no, look at Eleanor!

*(*Arthur *enters, helping* Eleanor *into the house. She has just come back from France and is not well. He gets her seated somewhere and she collapses back into the chair, relieved to be home)*

Eleanor: Just get me some water.

*(*Maria *goes to do this.* Arthur *heads back outside to get the rest of the luggage, etc.* Catherine *enters, carrying some things, also back from France.)*

Catherine: Mother?

Eleanor: I'm just so glad to be home.

Catherine: I called one of her colleagues at the hospital. They want to see her immediately.

Eleanor: No. I'm sleeping in my own bed for a night before anyone sees me. I'm a doctor and I know what I'm doing.

LAVINIA: Eleanor?

ELEANOR: Liv. Can you help me upstairs in a bit? And then sleep in my room? Catherine needs a break.

LAVINIA: *(Crying)* Oh, Eleanor…

CATHERINE: I'm fine, Mother.

ELEANOR: *(To* CATHERINE*)* That dress looks so good on you.

CATHERINE: Thank you.

ELEANOR: We got some lovely clothes In Lyon. Lavinia, stop crying.
Their shopping is almost as good as in Paris. Cathy was very good. Her French is—

LAVINIA: I am just so concerned about you, Ellie!

ELEANOR: Look at me. I'm fine. I just need rest.

CATHERINE: My French was all right. It was good enough to translate most of what you needed. But I was lacking in vocabulary.

ELEANOR: You were…more than satisfactory.

CATHERINE: Thank you, Mother.
Aunt Lavinia, stop crying. It's not helping. In general, I would say that tears do not help any situation.

*(*ARTHUR *enters with the rest of the luggage.)*

ELEANOR: I hope you tipped him well, Arthur. You didn't skimp, did you?

ARTHUR: No, Ellie.

CATHERINE: *(Having grabbed some of the mail from the study)* Oh, Mother, your mail—

ELEANOR: Sort it for me, will you? And we can discuss it tomorrow. Now I'm ready to go upstairs.

*(*ARTHUR *and* CATHERINE *start to help* ELEANOR *upstairs.* LAVINIA *takes over.)*

ARTHUR: How bad was it?

CATHERINE: It started as one of her headaches and then she couldn't breathe. The doctors in Lyon weren't going to let her come home yet, but they did an X-ray and decided she needed to get to her own doctors.

ARTHUR: So, what is it?

CATHERINE: She's going to need heart surgery.

ARTHUR: So they found she had a heart, after all.

CATHERINE: Arthur. This is my mother.

ARTHUR: Sorry.

CATHERINE: She has tried very hard after—you know.

ARTHUR: We were all worried about you.

CATHERINE: Well, don't worry about me any more.

ARTHUR: I do love your mother, Cathy.

CATHERINE: Well, why don't you marry her and take care of her, Arthur.

ARTHUR: She won't let anyone take care of her.

CATHERINE: That's not true, anymore. She's changed.

ARTHUR: You think people can change. I'm not sure about that.

CATHERINE: I've changed, Arthur. That little girl who sat by that doorway and waited and waited? Until the morning sun coming In the window woke her up? She's gone. Forever. Catherine Sloper is here. Hello.

(CATHERINE *puts out her hand.* ARTHUR *takes it, bends down to kiss it.*)

CATHERINE: I prefer a handshake, sir.

ARTHUR: Oh, alright, then. Madamoiselle.

CATHERINE: I'm not kidding!

LAVINIA: (*Coming downstairs, speaking to* MARIA) Dr Sloper needs you to help her into bed. My back...

(MARIA *goes upstairs.* LAVINIA *speaks to* CATHERINE.)

LAVINIA: Cathy, sweetheart. You look wonderful. Arthur? Could you leave us alone, please?

ARTHUR: Tell Ellie I'll be back later.

(ARTHUR *leans in to kiss* CATHERINE *on the cheek. She lets him*)

ARTHUR: Finally, someone lets me kiss them. I am glad you're home. And the same for your mother.

CATHERINE: Good-bye, Arthur.

LAVINIA: Good-bye.

(ARTHUR *waves and exits.*)

(*Long beat*)

LAVINIA: Have you seen the mail?

CATHERINE: I don't want to know, Aunt Liv.

LAVINIA: Why not?

CATHERINE: There's nothing he could say.

LAVINIA: Here.

(LAVINIA *hands* CATHERINE *a letter.* CATHERINE *looks at it, see postmark*)

CATHERINE: California. I don't even want to see—I'm sorry I saw even—THAT!! Get it away from me.

LAVINIA: Cathy...

CATHERINE: No.

LAVINIA: Honey...I'm old enough to know how precious love can be.

CATHERINE: Love???? Love???? (*She takes the letter and tears it up and throws it away*). How can you upset me like this? I just got back from a wonderful trip with

my mother. Where she needed me. She treated me
like an adult. She came to depend on me! I had gotten
away from the horrible pain of that day and the next
morning. And now, I'm back in this house for two
minutes and you hit me with this! This…heartbreak,
Aunt Lavinia. Like taking a baseball bat and hitting a
wound that has finally healed. Are you so attached to
this idea of movie love, all that romantic crap that you
think you had with your husband, who's been dead
for twenty years, okay? Twenty years! He's dead, Aunt
Liv! Dead! And so is my love for Morris!
His name. Kills. Me.

LAVINIA: People are complicated, Cathy.

CATHERINE: Are you making excuses for him?

LAVINIA: No.

CATHERINE: Then what are you doing?

LAVINIA: I'm sorry you tore up that letter.

CATHERINE: Why? Mother's right.

LAVINIA: What do you mean?

CATHERINE: That you need pretty stories to live in, that
reality is too real for you, that you are a sentimental old
lady.

LAVINIA: I believe in love. I have faith in it.

CATHERINE: And that's what you think that letter
contains? Love?

LAVINIA: Why else would he have written it?

CATHERINE: To make himself seems less of a bastard. If
only to himself. I can see him— (Stricken with his image)

LAVINIA: What, dear?

CATHERINE: I don't want to see him. I've tried to forget
what he looked like.

LAVINIA: I'm sorry, dearest—

CATHERINE: No, you're not. You're living off of this.

LAVINIA: Cathy, no.

CATHERINE: Yes. You need this. Well, here it is: I can see him mailing this to me and saying to himself, "There", as if that settles everything. I loved him. He made love to me. I cannot forget what it felt like. I thought, "this is what married people have. And they take it for granted. And they let stupid things, money, petty fights, get In the way of it. And they lose it. This is what lovers have. And think they will have it always."

LAVINIA: I am so sorry.

CATHERINE: I could've gotten pregnant. In a way, I did. And then it died. Inside me. A baby made of stone. And it's heavy, carrying it around. And it's stupid. And dumb. And dead. And I will just have to live with it. And I'm learning how. So I never want to talk about this again. Aunt Lavinia. Never.

(LAVINIA *just nods in assent.*)

CATHERINE: And now I'm going to go check on my mother.

(MARIA *enters from upstairs, hurriedly.*)

MARIA: Miss? I think you'd better call the ambulance.

LAVINIA: (*Hurrying to and up the stairs*) Eleanor!

CATHERINE: (*Going to the phone, dialing, afraid her mother's illness has escalated*) Oh god.

(*End of Scene One*)

Scene Two

(Two years later, ARTHUR enters the house without knocking. The living room has been set up to accommodate a sick person—ELEANOR. He hangs up his hat? and coat, goes into the study, comes out with some papers, puts them down, crosses into the kitchen, comes out with the ice bucket for the bar, proceeds to make himself a martini.)

MARIA: *(Entering)* Oh, Mr Townsend! It's you.

ARTHUR: I've had my own key ever since Eleanor and Catherine came back from Europe and your mistress had her stroke. That's two years ago. I would think, Maria, that you could focus your attention on the many other things that need to be done around here instead of policing the door.

MARIA: I'm sorry, Mr Townsend.

ARTHUR: You make me feel like an intruder when you're shocked to see me.

MARIA: I'm not shocked. I—well—the other Mr Townsend has been coming by. And he has the habit of walking in.

ARTHUR: "Walking in"?

MARIA: He waits, I think. Until the door is open. He did that before.

ARTHUR: "Before"?

MARIA: With the flowers.

ARTHUR: He sent flowers? When? Has Miss Catherine seen him?

MARIA: No, the flowers were years ago, when they first met. The flower boy said that he, the flower boy, was delivering more than one vase of flowers, which he, the flower boy, did, and then to leave the door open because he—

ARTHUR: I get it.

MARIA: *(Says it, anyway, but slowly because she can only slow herself down, not change her train of thought)* —the flowwwwerrrr boy was coming back for his tip but he—

(Stops herself because she knows ARTHUR doesn't want her to repeat "the flower boy")

ARTHUR: "The flower boy"

MARIA: —didn't come back but Mr Townsend, not you, Mr Townsend, but the other Mr Townsend, just walked in.

ARTHUR: I need to talk to you, Maria. Sit down.

MARIA: Oh, I couldn't.

ARTHUR: I give you permission. Sit.

(MARIA sits.)

ARTHUR: Now, let's take it step-by-step. No, that's too complicated because it involves the past and the past seems as present to you as the present.

MARIA: What?

ARTHUR: You seem to remember the past so clearly.

MARIA: I see everything, Mr Townsend. That is part of my job. But I never talk about it. Except when someone is hurting.

ARTHUR: Like Catherine?

MARIA: Yes.

ARTHUR: All right. For her sake, just tell me about Mr Townsend's most recent visits?

MARIA: Well, they're not really visits because I don't let him in. Dr Sloper has forbidden any contact with Catherine, Miss Catherine, and I am not going to go against Dr Sloper.

ARTHUR: What if Miss Catherine wanted to see him?

MARIA: She doesn't.

ARTHUR: You don't like Mr Townsend.

MARIA: I never did. I knew he wouldn't come back
for her. And I told her, but she didn't believe me. I
knew I was right, but, by morning, I didn't want to
be but I *was* right. I had watched her all through that
awful night and I'd put a blanket around her after she
fell asleep on her luggage. If that wasn't the saddest
picture. And it's been her life. Always being sent away.
To some school or other. Her and her luggage.

ARTHUR: How often has Mr Townsend—Morris—how
often has Morris been by and how long has it been
going on?

MARIA: Twice a week. For about six months.

ARTHUR: And Catherine doesn't know.

MARIA: I haven't told her.

ARTHUR: Has he written to her?

MARIA: Yes.

ARTHUR: And where are the notes?

MARIA: They are letters.

ARTHUR: Cathy goes through the mail since she
handles all of her mother's affairs now.

MARIA: Dr Sloper has me get to the mail first. That's
another reason I watch the door.

(LAVINIA *enters from upstairs,* MARIA *jumps up, guilty
because she's sitting down*)

LAVINIA: Maria, you're needed.

(MARIA *heads upstairs.*)

ARTHUR: Lavinia.

LAVINIA: Arthur.

(CATHERINE *enters from the kitchen. She is dressed in some "hip" trousers. She's discovered her own shopping places.*)

CATHERINE: Is she up?

ELEANOR: *(From upstairs)* Cathy!! Where have you been?

(CATHERINE *doesn't answer. From her bedroom to the top of the stairs,* ELEANOR *emerges, helped by* MARIA.)

ELEANOR: Maria! Stop!

MARIA: What?

ELEANOR: Whatever you're doing. It's not helping. Cathy! There you are! Why didn't you answer me?

CATHERINE: Didn't we agree to use our indoor voices, Indoors? Mother?

ELEANOR: You've been reading Dr Spock's *Guide to Infant Care* or whatever that seditious book is called and trying to apply it me. Because you think of me as a child. Well, I am not a child. I am recovering from an illness, and—MARIA, STOP HELPING ME!!

(ARTHUR *downs his martini and starts upstairs*)

ARTHUR: Ellie—quiet down. You're all right.

ELEANOR: *(To* ARTHUR*)* And now you're patronizing me.

ARTHUR: *(To* MARIA*)* Bring her pillow.

(ARTHUR *gently picks* ELEANOR *up and carries her downstairs. She puts her head on his shoulder. He carries her to the chair or couch where she usually sits and puts her down carefully.* MARIA *follows with the pillow. They set* ELEANOR *up. No one speaks. It's a routine. And* ELEANOR *allows* ARTHUR *to help her*)

CATHERINE: Hello, Mother.

ELEANOR: What are you wearing? Lavinia, look at what this child is wearing.

LAVINIA: Trousers. Like Kate Hepburn.

ELEANOR: No. These are something else, entirely.

CATHERINE: I delivered those summaries to your office. It's silly to mail them paperwork daily. The insurance claims are becoming more and more complicated. I think you should hire someone to do just those. Not me, though.

ELEANOR: I miss obstetrics.

CATHERINE: Well, you could—

ELEANOR: I am not retiring! That makes me an invalid. "IN VALID" is what that means.

CATHERINE: I meant, you could lecture.

ELEANOR: Teach, is what you mean.

CATHERINE: No, I would have said, "teach", if I had meant that. Yale-New Haven sent you that letter.

ELEANOR: I spend three days a week, either sitting on this couch, in bed—

ARTHUR: In physical therapy.

ELEANOR: Yes, Arthur.

LAVINIA: Taking walks with me and Maria.

ELEANOR: I have helpers everywhere. Little elves to help me get better.

CATHERINE: Attitude change, Mother. Calmer. Quieter.

ELEANOR: And when I get to work, which I appreciate, In the office, seeing patients, which I also appreciate having, I spend those rare days face-to-face with the, as my mother used to call it, the "front-bottom" parts of women. I am, I have become, a gynecologist. A mere gynecologist, when I used to deliver babies, save babies, save women, as their most dangerous moments, the riskiest thing they will do In their lifetimes.

CATHERINE: You're lucky to be alive, Mom.

ELEANOR: "Lucky"??? Luck has never been a part of my life. Work. That has sustained me. And made this life you have. My work. That is my answer to whomever is handing out the luck. "Don't do me any favors, Mr Luck, you...S-O-B—"

ARTHUR: (Hushing her) Eleanor...sh...sh...sh...

ELEANOR: Can we call this meeting to order? Lavinia, we're going to talk about money, and that may frighten you...

(LAVINIA exits.)

CATHERINE: All right. I've sorted through most of what the accountant sent us and I have no questions, Arthur. He incorporated all of my notes, so this can go back to you, and then come back to Mother and she will sign. My paperwork is ready for the I R S. But you'll want to check it. Won't you?

ARTHUR: I'll look at it, of course. But I'm sure... Eleanor, are you all right?

ELEANOR: Oh, can I have a drink, please? Please, Cathy? A little gin with a ceremony of Vermouth?

CATHERINE: Your doctor prefers that you drink wine.

ELEANOR: I hate wine. It's for pretenders.

CATHERINE: Oh, all right. (Checks the time) It's a little early.

ELEANOR: I declare the cocktail flag as up.

ARTHUR: Cathy. It's always four P M on Washington Square.

CATHERINE: Why am I the publican all of a sudden?

ELEANOR: Because you're the adult in this house.

CATHERINE: Mommy. Thank you.

(CATHERINE *goes to* ELEANOR *and gives her a genuine hug.*)

ELEANOR: I depend on you. For so much.

(ARTHUR *goes to make a martini for* ELEANOR.)

ARTHUR: And I'll let the gin read the label on the vermouth. And we're done.

ELEANOR: *(Whispering to* CATHERINE*)* I promise I won't get sloshed.

CATHERINE: I won't let you.

(They drink.)

ELEANOR: Now. We have to do this. I know no one here wants to talk about…these things…but it must be done. Arthur?

ARTHUR: *(Takes out some papers, goes through them)* Now, my advice is for Eleanor to sign over to Catherine all of Eleanor's assets, to avoid probate and inheritance taxes. I've got the paperwork here. As executor, I've already signed. This new will cannot, not would your mother want to, change your inheritance from your father, which continues to supply you with ten thousand a year until you are thirty.

CATHERINE: At which time, I will be working full-time.

ELEANOR: You're going back to school!

CATHERINE: No. I'm starting a business. I'm going to be catering.

ELEANOR: What is—? You mean, those people who—

CATHERINE: —make food for other people. Yes, Mother.

ELEANOR: *(This is suspect—blue-collar job)* They don't have a union, do they?

CATHERINE: They do. But I would only join if I worked for someone else. Like at a big hotel.

ELEANOR: So you would be in charge?

CATHERINE: Yes. It will be my business. And I will be in charge. Maria may be my first employee.

ELEANOR: Arthur?

ARTHUR: I think it's a splendid idea.

ELEANOR: How many martinis have you had?

ARTHUR: This is my second. But I thought it was a good idea at coffee last week.

ELEANOR: Are you keeping things from me?

ARTHUR: Ellie. Stop it.

ELEANOR: What if you get married, Catherine?

CATHERINE: I'm not going to get married, Mother.

ELEANOR: You don't know that.

CATHERINE: Oh yes. I do.

ELEANOR: You don't know, Cathy. So I've asked Arthur to put into the will, this stipulation: That you will never marry Morris Townsend.

CATHERINE: What?

ARTHUR: Your mother has put specific wording into her will that you will inherit nothing if you were to marry Morris—

CATHERINE: Morris Townsend? I never think about him anymore. It's been—how long has it been? Two years. Goodness. *(Relief. She shakes her head in amazement.)* And I thought I was going to die. And I didn't. In fact, life is so good now.

ELEANOR: He had such power over you.

CATHERINE: Well, I was in love with him.
And I was so young. But he was so cruel, Mother.

ARTHUR: See, Ellie? There's nothing to worry about.
And no need to rewrite the other document.

ELEANOR: She admits she was in love with him.

CATHERINE: I'm not anymore. How could I be?

ELEANOR: Love is stronger than anything, stronger than
anger, even hate. Miguel betrayed me. And I hated
him. But only for a while. And then the love returned.
And I will die, loving him, still. Arthur—

ARTHUR: What.

ELEANOR: I'm sorry. I will always love Miguel.

ARTHUR: About what?

ELEANOR: Oh, I forgot. You don't care.

CATHERINE: Daddy betrayed you?

ELEANOR: Oh, you know: MEN.

CATHERINE: I can't believe that. *(Remembers* MORRIS*)* Oh
yes, I can. Of course, I can. My daddy was like Morris?
I can't stand it. How are women supposed to live In the
world when men are such…cruel…pretenders!

ELEANOR: Your father wasn't a pretender. He loved
me. He loved me more than anyone else in the world.
He was in love with me. He just…some women are so
forceful with handsome men. And men have this…
response. And they can't help themselves. It takes over
and they can't—

CATHERINE: Mother…?

ELEANOR: I am protecting you, Catherine, from
yourself. And your feelings. Feelings can ruin a
woman's life.

ARTHUR: Ellie, this may not be the time. I don't want
your blood pressure to soar.

ELEANOR: No, this has to be done. Now.

I want Catherine to promise me she won't marry Morris Townsend. I want her to sign something.

CATHERINE: What?
Mother, this is silly.

ELEANOR: I want you to write, "I will never marry Morris Townsend," and sign it.

CATHERINE: Mother, I…won't do that.

ARTHUR: Oh, Cathy, don't upset her. Just do it. I'll write it up.

ELEANOR: No, I want Catherine to write, "I will never marry Morris Townsend," and then sign it, here, in front of us.

CATHERINE: I'm not a little girl, anymore.

ELEANOR: I know that.

CATHERINE: Mother, I'm not going to write anything and sign it like I was nine years old and made a mistake. I did nothing wrong. I was the one who was wronged.

ELEANOR: Then, you won't have any problem doing this.

ARTHUR: You're upsetting your mother, Catherine. Just do what she wants.

CATHERINE: Arthur? You think this is stupid.

ARTHUR: It's what she wants. And she's—not well, Cathy.

CATHERINE: No. I won't be held hostage by what my mother wants. That was my entire life when I was a child. And too late into my adulthood. (To ELEANOR) You said yourself, Mother, that I am the adult in this household!

ELEANOR: Arthur—call Maria…

CATHERINE: What is it, Mother.

ELEANOR: I have to go to the toilet.

(CATHERINE *goes to help.* ELEANOR *repels her*)

ELEANOR: Arthur—

(ARTHUR *picks* ELEANOR *up and carries her.*)

ELEANOR: I'll have to use the one off the kitchen.

(ARTHUR *heads towards the kitchen.*)

ELEANOR: Did you ever think—

ARTHUR: It's all right, Eleanor.

ELEANOR: I love you, Arthur. So much.
Can you say you love me? Just once?
We'll be alone. In the toilet. And then I'll know that
you mean it.

(*They exit*)

(LAVINIA *enters.*)

LAVINIA: What happened?

CATHERINE: (*Goes towards the kitchen*) Mother! Mommy,
let me help!

ELEANOR: (*Offstage*) No! Go away!

(*Sound of bathroom door shutting*)

LAVINIA: Is Arthur in there with her?
Well, that's a new one.
This world… (*She sits and goes back to her knitting.*) Have
you heard about macramé, Cathy? It's all the rage.

(*End of Scene Two*)

Scene Three

(One year later. The front door to the outside is open. Phone rings, but nobody answers. It stops ringing. MARIA *enters, carrying a large tray, catering size, of hors d'oeuvres. The phone begins to ring again. She can't find a place to put the large tray down so that she can answer the phone. She heads back into the kitchen with the huge tray, re-enters to answer the phone. The phone stops ringing. She stands and looks at the phone for a beat, waiting for the person to call back. She then heads back into the kitchen, gets the tray she took there, and re-enters with it and, of course, the phone starts ringing agaIn)*

MARIA: *(Yelling to* CATHERINE *who is in the garden)* The station wagon is here. It's outside. I'm carrying the last tray out to them right now. *(She exits outside with the tray.)*

(Beat. No one on stage)

(Through the open front door, MORRIS *enters. He looks like an early hippie, but well-dressed, In a Nehru jacket, tight pants, Beatle boots)*

*(*MARIA *re-enters from the outside, sees* MORRIS*)*

MARIA: Uh-oh.

MORRIS: Hello, Maria.

*(*MARIA *just sighs.)*

MORRIS: I hope I'm welcome.

MARIA: It's not my place, sir. *(Calling out)* Miss Catherine?

CATHERINE: *(Offstage)* I got the ramekins off the garden. They cooled enough to set up. And that finishes this order. Maria, you don't need to go.

(CATHERINE *enters with the ramekins, ready for the station wagon, stops when she sees* MORRIS. MARIA *takes them from her and heads outside with them.)*

MORRIS: I just saw Arthur. At his office.

(Phone rings)

CATHERINE: *(On the phone)* Hello.

Yes.

Yes, he's here.

Would you like to speak with him?

I'm fine.

Good-bye, Arthur.

Good—

I said, good-bye. *(She hangs up the phone.)*

MORRIS: I told Arthur I was coming over today and that I was going to see you.

*(MARIA *enters from the outside, shuts the front door)*

MARIA: Shall I get...someone? Your Aunt Lavinia?

CATHERINE: No, Maria. You're off-duty now.

*(MARIA *doesn't want to leave)*

CATHERINE: You may go, Maria.

*(Unsure of where to exit, MARIA *chooses to go upstairs)*

CATHERINE: *(To MARIA)* Don't disturb Aunt Liv. She's watching her soaps in her room.

*(MARIA *stays at the top of the stairs.)*

CATHERINE: Go to your room, Maria.

*(MARIA *comes downstairs and goes to her room.)*

MORRIS: You look so different. It's so good to see you. And I can tell you in person how sorry I am about your mother's death.

CATHERINE: No, you're not.

MORRIS: I respected her, Catherine. I did.

CATHERINE: I didn't inherit her money, Morris. I
did get the house and I still have a few years of the
inheritance from my father. The parent that never
knew me or even that I existed is the one who took care
of me. In the end. I know that's why you're here—to
find out if I am a rich woman. Well, I'm not.

MORRIS: I don't care about that. I never did.

CATHERINE: I don't believe you. And now you need to
go.

MORRIS: I tried to explain myself in the letter. You
never wrote back.

CATHERINE: The letter? Oh, that letter. I didn't read it,
Morris.

MORRIS: You didn't even read it? You never read it? At
all?

CATHERINE: By the time it arrived. Instead of you. I
had no interest in reading anything you had to say.
So I tore it up, and then began putting myself back
together. As you can see, I did a nice job of putting
myself back together. The thing is, Morris, I put
myself back together in a new way. I am the new and
improved Catherine Sloper.

MORRIS: (Quoting the letter) "Dearest Cathy," I wrote. "I
know you must be furious with me and I don't blame
you, my dear Lady—"

CATHERINE: "Lady"!

MORRIS: From Lady and the Tramp. You remember.

CATHERINE: (Realizing how young she was) I was a baby.
(It hits her—his crime) You made love to a baby and
then left her!!

MORRIS: *(Continuing with his reciting of the letter)* And then I said, "But I couldn't go through with our plans." And then, I wrote—see? I remember it, verbatim.

CATHERINE: "Our plans"? I had no plan. I fell in love with you. You took my virginity. And then you decided we were going to get married.

MORRIS: You seduced *me*.

CATHERINE: I was a child. I took you to my bedroom. Is that seduction?

MORRIS: For a young man—yes! And you were nineteen years old!

CATHERINE: I was still a child.

MORRIS: Well, your body wasn't. Believe me. You were and still are a very…fully-grown woman.

CATHERINE: You're six years older than I am!

MORRIS: That doesn't mean I was grown up! I was in love, too.

CATHERINE: With me?

MORRIS: Yes. What did you think? That I was faking everything?

CATHERINE: You left! And because somehow you knew that my mother wasn't going to give me her money when she died.

Did you? Know that.

MORRIS: Yes. But that's not why—

CATHERINE: How did you know that? Did Arthur tell you?

MORRIS: No.

Your mother made it clear to me that I wasn't worthy of this family, of you. And that all I wanted was the money. So I couldn't—my pride would not let me just accept that.

CATHERINE: Your pride? What does that mean?

MORRIS: We are not the same, Cathy. You have grown up with privilege. And I have had to worry daily about would I have enough money to take the subway.

CATHERINE: But you had Arthur.

MORRIS: Unless you have your own money. You have nothing. Nothing. You're always there with your hand out.

CATHERINE: But the night of the party. You bought that liquor.

MORRIS: Courvasier cognac. Arthur gave me the money for that. I took the subway home, while those other "young people" from Arthur's office arrived in a taxi. I didn't want them to see me so I ducked out the back, after you left me standing there.

CATHERINE: I was frightened. And with good reason, as it turns out.

MORRIS: Oh, why are there all these problems? I love you, Cathy. And I believe you love me.

CATHERINE: You left me, Morris. Without a word.

MORRIS: I wrote you a letter.

CATHERINE: You're always writing things to me. Why can't you ever just show up and say them to me?

MORRIS: Because I wasn't allowed to see you. Because your mother made certain I knew that I wasn't worthy of you and of this family. The Slopers. Your mother's very white family.

CATHERINE: White?

MORRIS: Because I am Black, Cathy.

CATHERINE: "Black." Oh, that word.

MORRIS: Yes. It replaced the other words.

CATHERINE: But you're not Black, you're light brown. Like me. Look.

MORRIS: And you're not worthy, either. You can't trust them.

CATHERINE: Who?

MORRIS: Everyone. Your Aunt Lavinia.

LAVINIA: *(She's been eavesdropping)* That's not true!

MORRIS: You're thinking it. You've always thought it.

LAVINIA: I didn't! That's—that's—a terrible accusation!

MORRIS: And my cousin Arthur. He sees us differently, too. And—well, not Maria. Because she's not white. I'm not sure what she is—

MARIA: *(Also eavesdropping)* I'm Italian. Excuse me.

CATHERINE: And you accepted my mother's judgment?

MORRIS: I wanted to prove, as a man, that I was capable of doing something on my own, that I was capable of earning a living and having social status.

CATHERINE: Why?

MORRIS: My name, "Townsend", has prestige, but I have one pair of shoes.

CATHERINE: And they are THOSE shoes?

MORRIS: There. You sound like your mother.

CATHERINE: She's dead, Morris.

MORRIS: Is she?
For your information, I have more shoes now because I have a job.

CATHERINE: Doing what?

MORRIS: SellIng shoes. Yes. I work in the Village at a clothing store. We sell used clothing. Like Levis. Men In the Village love to wear the 501s. And we have India print shirts and dresses. And trousers made of velvet. Tight trousers. It's the kind of job your mother would have laughed at. That's what has kept me away.

CATHERINE: My mother's dead, Morris. She has been dead for over a year. What really kept you away?

MORRIS: You wouldn't see me! I don't blame you. But I thought my letters would win you over. And I came by every few days, but I didn't even get a glimpse of you.

CATHERINE: You came by?

MORRIS: Yes.

(LAVINIA *tries to escape subtlely.*)

MORRIS: And I wrote letters. But nothing from you. And I don't blame you—I know you were so hurt. And I didn't handle anything well. But I loved you, then, Cathy. And I still do.

CATHERINE: Aunt Lavinia?

LAVINIA: Maria?

MARIA: *(Appearing)* It was me, Miss. I'm sorry.

CATHERINE: What?

MARIA: Your mother asked me to get the letters before you saw them.

CATHERINE: I did the mail.

MARIA: I got to it first. Because your mother wanted—

CATHERINE: "Wanted" —my mother "wanted". And she always got what she wanted, didn't she?

LAVINIA: No. Or she would have been happy.

MORRIS: What happened to my letters?

MARIA: Dr Sloper got rid of them.

CATHERINE: But Dr Sloper has been gone. For some time now. Who got rid of them after she died? You just stopped trying, didn't you, Morris?

MORRIS: How long was I supposed to hit my head against a wall? I have some pride, Cathy.

CATHERINE: I'm glad. Because you left me with none. I had to find it. On my own. But I did. Find it. Morris.

MORRIS: I am so sorry about that night. I was scared, Cathy. And angry. I was so angry.

CATHERINE: Angry!?

MORRIS: Because your mother didn't think I was man enough to take care of you. Ever.

CATHERINE: What did it mean to you what *she* thought?

MORRIS: Everything. Because you can't help but see the world her way.

CATHERINE: You think I'm that shallow?

MORRIS: I thought and I still think you're that innocent. Look at this house. It's like a fortress against reality.

CATHERINE: It's a house you want.

MORRIS: Yes. I do want it.

CATHERINE: There's never been any hope. For us.

(ARTHUR *enters.*)

ARTHUR: I came as soon as I could.

CATHERINE: I'm not in any danger, Arthur.

ARTHUR: Morris, what are you doing here?

MORRIS: I finally got to see her on my own. Everyone has been conspiring against that!

CATHERINE: Arthur, were you trying to keep us separated?

ARTHUR: Your mother—I wanted her to be happy. She was so ill.

CATHERINE: You've always been my father, Arthur. How could you betray me like that?

ARTHUR: I had to choose—between your mother and you.

CATHERINE: But I'm the one with the future.

ARTHUR: Well, he's here now.

MORRIS: Cathy...

(MORRIS *crosses to* CATHERINE *and kisses her. It affects her. He kisses her again.*)

CATHERINE: How many women have you been with, Morris?

MORRIS: What? When?

CATHERINE: Since you kissed me last.

MORRIS: You mean two years ago?

CATHERINE: Yes.

MORRIS: Well, I haven't been celibate. I'm a man. It's not normal for a man to be celibate. But I have always loved you.

CATHERINE: So you haven't loved the other girls.

MORRIS: Uh...

CATHERINE: That seems cruel. To make love to a girl and not love her. Are they heart-broken? Afterwards?

MORRIS: Not everyone's like you, Cathy.

CATHERINE: How is that? You mean, a virgin? A young woman who falls in love with a man who says he loves her? Tell me because I want to understand.

MORRIS: Catherine. You are so young.

CATHERINE: Not as young as I was then.

MORRIS: The world isn't—

CATHERINE: What?

MORRIS: Pretty. And pure. And always true.

CATHERINE: You made me believe I'm pretty. And
what we had was pure. And I thought you were true.
And now I believe, In fact, that I am all those things. So
thank you for that.

MORRIS: You are, but real life is so much more
complicated.

CATHERINE: We need to ask more of life, then. We need
to keep our standards high, and not settle.

MORRIS: Oh, Cathy…you need me to protect you from
so much that is going to come your way.

CATHERINE: No. No, I think I'm saying good-bye,
Morris.

MORRIS: This isn't going the way I wanted it to. I love
you. I'm the one who needs you in my life. Cathy,
please….

CATHERINE: Arthur?

ARTHUR: Morris, let's go. Come on, son. Let's go.

(MORRIS *crosses to* CATHERINE *and kisses her passionately
one last time. She is affected by it.*)

CATHERINE: Go away.

MORRIS: You will work until you drop. Just like your
mother.

(MORRIS *exits.* ARTHUR *stays.*)

LAVINIA: Cathy—

CATHERINE: Stay away from me.
Arthur?

ARTHUR: Yes?

CATHERINE: Is he gone?

ARTHUR: Yes.

CATHERINE: You may go, too.

ARTHUR: You're all right?

CATHERINE: Oh, for heaven's sake, of course I'm all right. I will always be all right. Follow Morris. Make sure he stays away.

(ARTHUR *exits.*)

CATHERINE: Aunt Liv?

LAVINIA: Yes, dear.

CATHERINE: Hug me now.

(LAVINIA *goes to* CATHERINE *and hugs her.*)

CATHERINE: You know, Mother was right. She won.

LAVINIA: How, dear?

CATHERINE: I have become her.

LAVINIA: Not completely, dearest. You aren't a bitch.

CATHERINE: Maria!?

(MARIA *enters.*)

CATHERINE: Make certain Morris is gone.

(MARIA *goes out the front door, checks, comes back in*)

MARIA: He's gone. But there are a lot of people in the Square.

CATHERINE: Again? Are the police going to come like they did when all the beatniks were singing out there?

MARIA: Maybe…

CATHERINE: What's happened?

MARIA: *(Reading the signs she can see out of the window)* They have signs. "Viet…Nam." What's that?

LAVINIA: Oh, what's happened now? The coloreds are upset. Some crazy Communist kills the President...

CATHERINE: It's that place we have troops now. Like Korea. Only everyone is a lot more angry about it. *(Beat)* I'm going to go out.

MARIA: On the square?

CATHERINE: Yeah. Maria, do you want to go?

MARIA: I'll go with you.

LAVINIA: No, girls. I'm happy here.

CATHERINE: More people are arriving. It's exciting!

(CATHERINE exits out the front door on to the Square. MARIA *follows her out and shuts the door behind them.* LAVINIA *looks out the window. The sounds of the protest grow.)*

LAVINIA: Be careful, dear!

(Lights go down on the living room of 2 Washington Square. LAVINIA *turns on one lamp, and sits to continue her needlework.)*

END OF PLAY